Quotations of Badshah Khan

Compiler & Translator: Dr. Yahya Wardak

Edition: first, 2022

Book Details

Book Title	Quotations of Badshah Khan (English)
Compiler & Translator	Dr. Yahya Wardak
Publisher	Afghanic
Copies	1000
Edition	First
Printed	2020
Download	www.afghanic.de/download www.ecampus-afghanistan.org

Printed in Germany

ISBN 978-3-942233-50-7

Preface for the First Edition

"Can you name any person, in the history of Afghanistan and the region, as a role model for you?" a journalist asked me during an interview for his magazine, eight years ago.[1]

My answer for the question was Khan Abdul Ghaffar Khan (Bacha Khan) though I had not known much about him, nor had I read writings of or about him. In the recent years, the more I studied about him, the more I became interested in him; this interest is getting more and more.

In my point of view, the value of Bacha Khan's personality is in the struggle he did against the main problems of the nation like violence, exchange marriage, illiteracy, extremism, negative competition and people's lack of information about religion.

Since these improper behaviors still exist in our society, the instructions of Bacha Khan do not only have historical value, but they are also a good solution of our problems. That is why my opinions regarding the issues are the same as his. Some of the ideas of him could be interesting for you too. If so, hopefully, you will benefit from and exercise them for the advantage of yourselves and your country.

I would like to thank Mr. Mubariz Sapai, Dr. Ramazan Saadat, Mr. Hedayatullah Bangish and Mr. Shah Jahan Kakakhil for providing me with references for this book. I also thank Mr. M.

[1] This brief interview was published on Ost-Westliches Journal, 3/2000

Reza Khan for providing me the relevant pictures. As well as, I thank Mr. Nasim Sabir for helping me in editing the book.

Hopefully, I will be able to compile more sayings of Bacha Khan and those of others on him, so that, I will share them with the readers.

Dr. Yahya Wardak, Bonn, Germany, November, 2008

Preface for the Third Edition

Five years ago, I compiled "Quotations of Badshah Khan" from various books and magazines and printed as a book, in Germany. Because of the need for it, the book was reprinted in the same form in Kabul and was offered to its interested readers, in 2009. Since it is currently not available in bookstores, it needs to be printed again.

In the recent years, I could find other books on Badshah Khan and used them as further references for adding more to the previous version; thus, the third edition contains nearly 30 percent more contents than the others. In addition, the chronology of Badshah Khan's life has been written at the end of the book in order for the readers to be informed about different events of his life.

It is reported on the media in Afghanistan almost every day about explosions, war or suicide attacks in which people get wounded or lose their lives. A main cause of such a situation is our people who want to satisfy their ambitions and reach to their social and political targets through violence. And this is a main cause of the three decades of war in our country, as well.

Badshah Khan paid attention to this vital issue, a hundred years ago, and he struggled for resolving that. But unfortunately, Afghans either do not have the knowledge about violence or do not work for eliminating it.

One of the purposes of publishing "Quotations of Badshah Khan" and other books about him is to make the society aware of nonviolence. Hopefully, the readers will read them carefully, understand them, think about them and take advantages of them in their personal and social lives.

Unluckily, Afghans, Muslims and other people are not aware of Badshah Khan's ideas and actions. He analyzed, examined and knew the Afghan and Islamic society, and for reforming its weaknesses, he worked successfully. He struggled for reducing his nation's problems throughout his life. He spread his ideas on peace, brotherhood, love and nonviolence everywhere.

Dr. Mohammad Cyrus, the head of Directorate of Religious Affairs in Turkey says, "The main problem of Muslims is that they do not live in accordance with their religion. Many Muslim leaders and scholars, instead of resolving problems, create problems."

We and our leaders are to be blamed for not getting awareness about Badshah Khan's thoughts and struggles and not following his path.

I hope some readers will get information about his wishes, desires and achievements so that they will inform others; thus, they will follow his path and encourage others too. Based on this hope, the book is offered to you.

At the end, I would like to thank those who have helped me in the third edition of this book. I thank Mr. Asif Samim for providing me extra references from his library in Kama. As well as, I appreciate the efforts of Mr. Javid Kotwal and Abdul Hadi Asar in editing the book.

Dr. Yahya Wardak

Istanbul, October, 2014

Preface for English & Pashto Version

Dear Reader,

It is worth being pleased for that having published the book "Quotations of Badshah Khan" in English and Pashto together, I offer you this book.

Though Ghaffar Khan lived a century ago, his ideas and struggles are still precious and even more invaluable than in his time, for our society's today and the future. Through nonviolence, Ghaffar Khan and Gandhi could bring about freedom to the Subcontinent and played a major role in encouraging Muslims and Hindus to live peacefully alongside each other. Recently, works of Ghaffar Khan have been published in English, Turkish, Arabic, German and Italian languages, and they are reported in the international press.

In his message on peace in 2017, Pope Francesco said:

"Resolute and real approaches have resulted in outstanding outcomes. Success of Mahatma Gandhi and Ghaffar Khan is unforgettable …"

The violence in our beloved country Afghanistan has been a main factor of ruin, poverty and people's misfortune in the last four decades. It is possible to get inspired by the ideas and approaches of Ghaffar Khan in terms of the current problems, conflict and violence; thus get closer to peace, prosperity and unity. Based on this reason, I try to publish, promote, translate and print various books about Ghaffar Khan.

In this respect, his autobiography entitled "My Life and Struggle" was published in both Pashto and Dari languages by National Center of Policy and Research (NCPR) at Kabul

University, with the fund of Civil Peace Service of GIZ, in 2016.

The book you are holding in your hands “Quotations of Badshah Khan in English and Pashto” is a compilation of different national and international references of different languages and has been printed with the financial support of GIZ’s Civil Pease Service program (ZFD).

Hereby, I would like to thank (ZFD) and its energetic officer in Afghanistan Mr. Obaidullah Tanha for supporting me in printing of this work.

Finally I would like to express my appreciation for the efforts of my colleagues Hekmatullah Aziz and Fazel Rahim Baryal for helping me in translation and editing of this book.

Hopefully, you will read this small but rich book, learn its lessons and effectively use it for welfare of the nation and country.

Yahya Wardak, Kabul / Bonn 2020

Table of Contents

Desire of Bacha Khan

I have a big dream and desire.

The status of my nation is like that of the flowers grown in a desert, while nobody takes care of them; thus, with the passage of some days, they are withered and faded. I want my nation to cooperate during the times of both grief and happiness.

I want that my people work together for the welfare of the nation based on equality. I want them to play their national role and find a fair position among other nations of the world through serving Allah and the humanity.

Eknath Easwaren. Nonviolent soldier of Islam, Page 77

Islam

I strongly believe that:

Islam is Action, Faith and Love.

To be a Muslim is about having no disguised aim. Quran clearly states that believing in the Almighty Allah and performing good deeds are enough for the rescue of a human.

A Man to Match His Mountains, Page 11

The True Muslim

The Prophet Mohammad (peace be upon him) teaches us that a true Muslim is he who works for the happiness and profit of the creatures of Allah the Exalted.

It is the requirement of the belief in Allah to love human beings.

A Man to Match His Mountains, Page 99

Non-violence, A New Belief?

To act upon the philosophy of non-violence for a Pashtoon or a Muslim is not strange.

It is not a new belief.

Rather, it was applied around fourteen hundred years ago in Mecca by the Prophet, and since then, is followed by all who want to get rid of cruelty.

But, we had forgotten this belief until Gandhi reminded us about that, and we assumed it as a new belief.

Nonviolent Soldier of Islam by Eknath Easwaren, Page 103

Bacha Khan: It is not worthy of being worried about; I am upset to repeatedly tell you Pashtoons, everywhere, not to use the means of violence.

If you want me to be happy, think again about what I said.

Honorable Memories of the Great Servant of God, Page 59

Corruption

I am here to spread the movement of Khudai Khidmatgar. My responsibility is to spread, while it is up to the people whether to accept or reject it. In relation to corruption, as our perspective is based on nonviolence, we do not use corruption against anyone who use it against us.

Rubies and Pearls, Page 12

A Mind Full of Violence

Our minds are full of violence; therefore, we cannot easily understand its concept.

Instructions and Articles of Bacha Khan, Page 26

Support of the Nation

We serve the nation for the sake of God.
If the nation support us, they will be free, otherwise if they oppose us, it will be detrimental for them.
It is because we cannot reach our goal without the nation's support.

My Life and Struggle, 539 page

Democracy

I believe that a nation will not have political wisdom unless they are socially stimulated and organized. And, democracy cannot be executed among the nation which lacks political wisdom.

Service of God, Page 19

Light

Pashtoons are a strong nation who can achieve benefits.
But, Pashtoons have two weaknesses:
- First, they are disunited.
- Second, they are weak against money.

If they mitigate these two weaknesses, no power of the world will dominate them.

Pashtoon Magazine, Issue# 8, 1992, Peshawar, Page 73

Pashtoons are a live nation, given that they have inspiring personalities. Unless a nation have motivational people, it will not be alive.

Rubies and Pearls, Page 26

Rebuild Your Home

Oh Pashtooons,
Your home has been destroyed. Stand up and rebuild your destroyed home!
And remember that you are part of a brave generation.

A Man to Match His Mountains, Page 40

The Shortcoming of My Nation

The history of my nation is full of stories about achievements and bravery.
But there is a disadvantage; what has been achieved with a great deal of sacrifice has been lost due to hostility and jealousy with each other.
They have suffered harm because of disunity among themselves.
No foreign power has overwhelmed them.

Can anyone confront them in the battlefield?

A Man to Match His Mountains, Page 55

Disappointment

I am not disappointed.

Disappointment is for those who work for themselves or their personal purpose and target.

I serve Pashtoons as a servant of God.

Why may I be disappointed?

A Man to Match His Mountains, Page 341

What We Want?

We want a name, a room in the home as well as to be the owner and builder of the room.

Ghaffar Khan: Non-violent Badshah of the Pakhtuns by Rajmohan Gandhi, Page 243

To Work

We should learn from all these sayings, and what we do should not be only based on emotions and feelings, rather we have to carefully think about any aspect of it.

And if we are not ready to bear any kind of sacrifice and hardship, we need not to begin the activity.

My Life and Struggle, Page 286

The Cruel

It is the truth that cruel people are not brave; they are very fearful and faithless.

A brave person is never cruel to others.

My Life and Struggle, Page 28

Patience

I want to equip you with a weapon against which police and army cannot do anything to you.

It is the weapon of our Prophet. It is the weapon of going straight on the way of patience and independence. No power of the world can defeat the power of this weapon.

When you visit your villages, tell the residents that you are the army of Allah the Exalted with the weapons of patience.

Recommend your brothers, relatives, and the villagers to join this army of Allah and bear all the hardship in this way.

If you have patience, you are going to be successful.

A Man to Match His Mountains, Page 223

The Habits of Childhood

The habits acquired in childhood will exist in the adulthood too; then it will be very hard to get rid of those bad habits.

My Life and Struggle, Page 18

Collapse of Governments

I am not here to talk about history. I just want to explain why Pashtoons could establish great governments but could not keep them up.

It was because Pashtoons lacked social life, love of nation and unity.

My Life and Struggle, Page 9

Success

Success requires social movement and sacrifice. Anyone who has such behaviors and feelings, they need to visit their nation and find followers with the same feelings to mutually confront cruelty and disrespect.

Once such a group comes into existence and organizes the nation, success can be gained, and nobody can then enslave the nation.

My Life and Struggle, Page 28

Fearful Nation

No fearful nation can survive in this world.

Rubies and Pearls, Page 17

Almsgiving

I have traveled to all of the Arabic countries. I have not witnessed such a way of almsgiving there, even in the holy cities of Mecca and Madina, as well as in Najaf and Karbala.

In those countries, when someone dies, people are invited and the dead body is carried to Masjid for offering the funeral prayer. Having prayed, the deceased person's relatives carry him/her to the graveyard for burial, and other people leave the area.

The religion of Islam has come to us from Saudi Arabia, but such bad traditions were introduced among us by selfish people.

My Life and Struggle, Page 40

Charity and Alms

As Islam has obliged us for charities and alms, there is a great secret in it. The beloved Prophet (peace be upon him) says that charity prevents calamity.

Do you know what this calamity is! It happens due to hatred between the poor and rich.

Once the rich people have sympathy with the poor and help them when they are in trouble, it will cause love between the poor and their rulers; thus resulting in preventing the calamity.

My Life and Struggle, Page 42

Competition

When people in a village of Pashtoons do something, people of another village will necessarily do the same for negative competition.

Rubies and Pearls, Page 11

Weakness of Human Beings

Human beings are such strange creatures. When they are weak and unable to do something, they seek various pretexts to hide their weakness and discouragement.

My Life and Struggle, Page 285

To Inspire Nations

Pashtoons are a live nation with the spirit of national love and sacrifice, but they need to be awakened. Nations are not inspired with invocation only.

To inspire and awake nations requires people who are selfless, pious, faithful and ready to serve their nation for the sake of God. Once such people come into existence in a nation, and love, sympathy, brotherhood and respect are created with their struggles, the nation will then improve.

Our fearful and selfish Khans, Mullahs and ancestors have kept us in darkness; therefore, we are in this current situation.

My Life and Struggle, Page 67

Weakness

It is a big weakness of Pashtoons that wherever they go and marry someone form that area, they forget their language.

Thousands of Hindus live here in the Frontier among us, but they have not forgotten their language. They speak Punjabi and have learnt our language too.

This weakness seems to be only among Pashtoons.

My Life and Struggle, Page 301

Bad Habit

It is to be sorry for that we are strict against who treats us in a good manner, while who beats us on heads, we stoop down for them; it is such a bad habit.
We need to quit such habits.

My Life and Struggle, Page 240

Taunts of People

My relatives and friends asked me many times why I travel on foot because people will backbite me.
We do many wrong works because of people's taunts.
I answered them that I don't care about what people say, rather I consider the work.
If the work is right, I do it in spite of whatever people say.
As well as, if it is a wrong work, I don't do it, no matter what people say.

My Life and Struggle, Page 158

Religion in Others' Language

The religions of Hindus and Muslims are in foreign languages. The religion of Hindus is in Sanskrit, and they don't know the language. As well as, our religion is in Arabic which we don't understand.

My Life and Struggle, Page 283

Ability to Do Something but Not Another

Since we cannot hide our weaknesses from God, we should not hide them from people either.

And, what we can do or not, we should obviously say that we are able or unable to do that.

Also, if another person is doing a good work, we should not say that we can't do it.

We should not oppose him, rather we should help him.

We should not cause dissension among our group or nation and should not blame them or create problems for them instead of encouraging them.

My Life and Struggle, Page 287

Respect

Any person's respect is due to himself.

If one controls his ambitions and wishes, he will always be relaxed, happy and respected.

My Life and Struggle, Page 300

Gun or Pen?

Nowadays, Pashtoons do not need gun, rather they need pen because our country's independence will be gained with pen, not gun.

Letters of Bacha Khan, Volume I, Page 43

Nation and Language

Indeed, Pashto had nothing and nobody cared about it. Pashtoons were as unwise and ignorant that they scorned their language. If a nation disrespects their language, they

themselves are disrespected. And if they lose their language, they themselves are lost.

My Life and Struggle, Page 334

Residents of the Hazara region are Pashtoons, but they have lost their language.

Rubies and Pearls, Page 12

Supplication

We call ourselves Muslims and are Pashtoons, but we kill, abash and spy on our Pashtoon Muslim brothers.

Supplicate that may God grant us wisdom and knowledge and add His love into our hearts, as well as create brotherhood, respect, love of nation and unity among us.

My Life and Struggle, Page 317

Fratricide

Oh Pashtoon brothers!

A nonbeliever does not kill his nonbeliever brother.

You call yourselves Muslims, but what is the reason that one Pashtoon kills another?

No English spies on his nation, rather he supports his nation. Also, one Hindu does not lie to testify against another Hindu.

Then Pashtoon brothers! Why do you state wrong testimony against each other and disrespect and abash each other?

Fear God and be ashamed of yourselves.

My Life and Struggle, Page 316

Leader?

People say that Pashtoons have not improved and are on the wrong path. In reality, has anyone guided them to the right path? Has anyone stopped them from the wrong path, but they have not avoided it?

I am sorry that they don't have a leader such as other nations do. They don't have a shepherd; thus, wolves bite and defeat them.

My Life and Struggle, Page 317

Service of God

We Pashtoons call a work or service as the service for God which is performed without any personal desire, purpose or wage just for the sake of God. Though God does not need to be served, to serve His creatures is actually service for Him.

My Life and Struggle, Page 356

Unlucky Nation

A nation of the world is very unlucky when its people are not ready for the service of their nation and country and even prevent others from offering services.

My Life and Struggle, Page 500

Jewish and Palestinians

Jewish have built new villages, cities and gardens in Palestine and are still building more, but Muslims are yet in ignorance, waiting for Imam Mahdi. They think that they should not do anything as Imam will come and do all for them.

They are as ignorant that they don't know that even if the Prophet, not Imam, were not supported by his nation, he would not have succeeded.

My Life and Struggle, Page 327

Our Land

God has bestowed this land on us the same as He has bestowed places on other nations for them and their children to live there.

This land is ours, but its authority is with others; thus, our children are hungry, thirsty and naked while others benefit from it.

My Life and Struggle, Page 506

Improvement of Nation

While I was in jail, I carefully thought about the situation of my nation.

I concluded that any nation in this world as well as knowledge and arts cannot improve without their own language.

I decided that I must begin publishing a Pashto magazine for educating my people, informing them about the world and directing them towards their language. As well as, I decided about an association that will provide primary education to the children in their native language.

My Life and Struggle, Page 333

Unfortunate Nation

As I see my unfortunate nation, at first, there is no one to serve them, then when anyone is here, people do not allow him to provide service.

My Life and Struggle, Page 453

Religions

Gandhi equally respected all religions. He considered all of them to be right, and I believe the same. God says in the Quran that He has assigned a guide to any nation among themselves.

My Life and Struggle, Page 686

Amanullah Khan and Revolution

There have been many kings among Pashtoons, but they had not loved any other king as much as both women and men loved Amanullah Khan.
Amanullah Khan would say that he was the revolutionary king of Pashtoons, and he was totally right about it as he caused an amazing revolution among Pashtoons.
Revolution is a flood which carries those who are sleeping, while awake people take its advantages.

My Life and Struggle, Page 341

Leaders and Nation

Bravery come into existence in any nation whose leaders are brave. And when a nation's leaders are fearful, the fear spreads among them.

My Life and Struggle, Page 728

First Speech of Badshah Khan in Duru

Pashtoon brothers! We are your brothers and your servants and have come for your service.

Let's rebuild our destroyed home!

Look at the world. If not knowledge, you have eyes. People and nations of the world rose to skies, but we remained on the face of earth.

They are also human beings like us, but we beg them; some for grain, some for money.

God has given us a country like Paradise, being full of property and blessings, but what our status is in it. We don't have even sufficient bread of maize to eat.

Why did they flourish? And why we remained backward? They live in brotherhood, love of nation and unity, while among us, there are divergence, parties, hatred, aversion and dissension. Today's world is a world of national unity. If you become a united nation, your world and the hereafter will flourish.

My Life and Struggle, Page 357

Patient People

God says: ask me for help with patience and unity.
God also says: those who are killed in the way of Allah are not dead. Rather, they are alive, but you don't perceive it. And God says: I am supporter of the patient people.

My Life and Struggle, Page 511

Political Wisdom

Political wisdom does not come to a nation from the sky.

When people having political wisdom emerge in a nation, they visit their nation to inspire the people with the wisdom.

Muslims are an outstanding nation, but such people have not emerged among them. Compare the leaders of Hindus and Muslims.

Leaders of Hindus are lovers of their nation.

But, Muslim leaders are *Khan Bahadar* and *Khan Sahib* [selfish Khans].

My Life and Struggle, Page 427

National Unity

Brothers! Today's world is based on national unity. You have witnessed that the nations with national unity and brotherhood rose to skies and flourished. We are also a nation, but why we remained backward.

We remained due to lack of national unity, brotherhood, love and harmony. I have come to you for you are my nation, but you have left your language, code of Pashtoonwali, civilization and everything; you even wear traditional clothing of others [as per imitation].

I would like to tell you that when a bird separates from flock, it will get lost.

My Life and Struggle, Page 438

Dissension

I believe that a nation with dissension and separate groups will not reach its goal.
And, as we are slaves, it is because of dissension and separated parties.
I hate separation into parties and dissension very much.

My Life and Struggle, Page 447

Every party is dissolved due to dissension.

Rubies and Pearls, Page 20

- Unless Pashtoons break the chains of slavery, they will not become eligible for competition with other nations of the world.

Rubies and Pearls, Page 17

There is no curse bigger than slavery.

Rubies and Pearls, Page 21

A slave has no religion or sect.

Rubies and Pearls, Page 30

Pashtoons, Become United!

We are a single nation and offspring of one ancestor.
We are as a tree with multiple branches and one stem. If one breaks a branch of this tree, it is only the shadow that decreases. But, if the stem is dried, all of the branches will dry.
Currently, English are gradually breaking the tree's branches.
Beware! If the branches are finished, your next generation will not survive as there will be no shadow on their heads. And, if the stem is dried, all branches will dry; no single one will remain.

My Life and Struggle, Page 455

I would like to remind you that the enemy is eradicating you, while trying to dry the stem.
If you let the stem dry, you will be lost.
Rise up!
Build your home; avoid the dissention; become one nation.
If you become a united nation, both of your world and the hereafter will be flourished.

My Life and Struggle, Page 456

I have one message and saying for you Pashtoons to become united, build your home and avoid separation, selfishness and

hostility so that you will have a glorious life in the hereafter as well as your world will be flourished and peaceful.

Rubies and Pearls, Page 35

Prosperity of Nation

When in a nation there is no one to serve for the sake of God, such nation will never improve in this world.
And when in a nation there in is no respect towards service, their country will never have prosperity.

Letters of Bacha Khan, Volume II, Page 47

Women

A nation cannot improve without [support of] women, because it is women who are responsible for raising children in our households.
Our vehicle has two wheels; one is man and the other is woman.
Suppose if one of the wheels is punctured, how will the vehicle move?

My Life and Struggle, Page 457

Unless the women of a nation are awakened, the entire nation is not awake.

Rubies and Pearls, Page 20

Service of God

God does not need to be served. To serve His creatures is service for God; his creatures are not the Muslims only, but also include all the humans whether Hindu, Sikh or Christian.

Our obligation is to eradicate cruelty from the world and rescue the oppressed form the cruel.

We will oppose any nation or government that oppress the God's creatures, no matter if the cruel is our brother and Muslim.

In addition, our service will be for God only, without any personal matter. No matter if anyone disturbs or oppresses us, we will not take revenge, rather we will be patient, trying to make the person, nation or government understand.

My Life and Struggle, Page 457

Nobody can prevent the action which is done for the sake of God.

Rubies and Pearls, Page 13

Purpose of the Movement

This is a movement of our brotherhood and national unity; thus, we try to gather all Pashtoons in brotherhood and unity and to remove hatred, aversion, hostility and enmity from their hearts so that they will become united with love and sympathy as a single nation.

My Life and Struggle, Page 458

The Main Purpose

We are also a nation. We also need to struggle for the prosperity and improvement of the nation. And if we spend all the life in poverty and slavery, we will be lost.
Our main purpose is to create love, national unity, brotherhood and harmony in the nation.

My Life and Struggle, Page 510

Your Land

Oh brothers!
You shall become a united nation as God has given you a land full of properties and blessings, but others take advantages of them because of your dissension. If you become a united nation, others cannot use your property.
In such a case, your world and life after death will be flourished, having a land where no single one will be poor; all will be Khans (wealth people).

My Life and Struggle, Page 458

Supplication and Action

A supplication without action is not acceptable for God.

Instructions and Articles of Bacha Khan, Page 11

Slavery is the curse from God, so we need to get rid of it. It is possible when there is national unity, brotherhood, harmony and love among us. I hope you will contemplate this saying of mine.

If there is only my benefit in it, do not act upon it; otherwise, if it is beneficial for your world and the hereafter, then do it so that you and your offspring will be prosperous.

My Life and Struggle, Page 506

Improvement

I believe that a nation can improve when its women stand for the service of their nation alongside men.

Rubies and Pearls, Page 20

Support Us

We have started serving the God's creatures for His sake.

If you also want to serve the God's creatures and want to satisfy God, then support us in the service of Him; this way, your world will change into paradise and will be deemed worthy of Paradise in the hereafter.

My Life and Struggle, Page 511

Putting Oneself Under Soil

Has a seed ever grown without being put under soil in land? Has it ever grown plants? Has it ever produced other seeds?

Seeds are always grown from the seed which is buried under the soil.

Letters of Bacha Khan, Volume I, Page 46

For Others

Why are we Pashtoons good for others but do nothing for ourselves?

Instructions and Articles of Bacha Khan, Page 15

A Free Book

I buy nothing for free, especially book and newspaper.

Honorable Memories of the Great Servant of God, Page 96

Cloths and Language of Our Own Country

One night all the women of village came together, and I and Hakim Sahib talked to them: unless you support the nation, it will not rise. I also made them promise to wear the domestic clothing.

My Life and Struggle, Page 516

Pashtoons of Hazara!

Remember this saying of mine that those who lost their language, they have lost themselves, and the ones who disrespect their language, they have been disrespected.
As you have lost your language, you have lost not only the language but also the Pashto [i.e. dignity].

My Life and Struggle, Page 514

War

Horses cannot be trained during the war.

Put yourself as a role model for them so that as you go forward, they will follow you.

Instructions and Articles of Bacha Khan, Page 14

Our Leader

You who raise your voice for making me a king, remember that our movement has not started for the purpose of ruling or to select me as the king.
Still if you elect me as the ruler, at first point, there is no kingship in Islam; in addition, you will become poor while I will be in comfort. So beware not to select me nor any other person as your king.
We don't want to have kings, and we don't need them either.
We will have a leader who will be selected by the votes and in consultation with the nation. It will be a person who is pious, faithful and sympathetic to the nation and country; a person who has suffered hardship and sacrifice while serving the nation and country.
This leader must also have the potential and knowledge of leadership.

My Life and Struggle, Page 527

Destroying the Country

The conflict in Afghanistan is a war between the USA and Russia, during which Pakistan is destroying itself for the interests of the USA.

Instructions and Articles of Bacha Khan, Page 21

Kingdom

Our government will be obedient to the community, not the vice versa.

Kingdom is something very bad, which is very harmful for the nation and country.

If there is a good king today, his son will accede to the power tomorrow. So, who can guarantee that the son will also be good? Also, kings do not want their nation to improve because they assume that if the public improves, they will be discharged; therefore, they always prevent the nation to get educated.

My Life and Struggle, Page 528

Words and Deeds

Remember this saying of mine!

The nations around the world who talk less but work more have always reached their goals.

I don't talk much; think about my advice!

My Life and Struggle, Page 367

Our Government

As this land belongs to all Pashtoons, we don't want one person to be Khan.

We will try to make all Khans and establish a government which will be based on equality, being beneficial and advantageous for all alike.

Whether it's bread or food without oil, it will be shared; there will be security and justice. All the nation will have a Jirga which will select the leader.

My Life and Struggle, Page 528

My Religion

My religion is truth, love and service of the God's creatures.

Religion has always brought the message of brotherhood and love to the world. The people whose hearts lack goodwill and love for the human beings and whose hearts are full of hatred, spite and rancor are distant from religion.

My Life and Struggle, Page 686

To Women

This land belongs to you the same as it does to men.
And as you think that men are higher than women, it is not the order of Islam; greatness is in action.
If a woman is morally good, righteous and virtuous, she is great, and the same is for men. Otherwise, if a woman is miscreant and misbehaving, she is low, and the same is true for men.
You have the same portion in this country as we do.
Women and men are like two wheels of a vehicle. If one of them is punctured, the vehicle cannot move forward.

My Life and Struggle, Page 530

Women and men have equal rights in this country.

Rubies and Pearls, Page 21

Women of the Nation

When women of a nation rise and struggle for the freedom of their nation, no one can enslave such a nation, and the nation will soon reach its target.

There is no national unity, brotherhood, love and unity.

When a nation opt for money, it then does not prefer relations and friendship.

Instructions and Articles of Bacha Khan, Page 18

Pashtoon women are more talented than men.

Rubies and Pearls, Page 43

Pashtoon Women

Our Pashtoon women are so pious, modest, loyal, and ready to serve. I always try to eliminate the feeling of underestimation from women's minds because it has been indoctrinated to them by selfish, ignorant men.

Instructions and Articles of Bacha Khan, Page 12

Women like milk cream and don't will to give it to someone because it will then cause lack in the quantity of butter.

Rubies and Pearls, Page 22

Marriage of Girls

Regarding those who arrange their girls' marriage in childhood or don't give them chance to select their life partner or prevent them from marriage, my advice is to quit this tradition. If all are not ready to quit it, at least the educated people should quit it; they should also educate their children before anything else.

Instructions and Articles of Bacha Khan, Page 27

This is a big disadvantage of my people that they enforce child marriage upon girls and don't let their girls to marry someone by their own wish; otherwise if they don't accept, they should not marry at all.

In this respect, I am of the opinion that this tradition also needs to be abandoned.

They need to first of all educate their children and pay special attention to their ethical education and training.

Once they pass studies, they should be helped with every means in dealings as per their wish.

Letters of Bacha Khan, Volume I, Page 16

Two Partners

The Almighty God has created man and woman as two partners for the prosperity of the globe. And, they are as two wheels of the vehicle of the humankind which cannot run with one wheel. Our Pashtoon women are so pious, lovely and loyal, besides willing to serve.

Instructions of Bacha Khan, Pages 20, 21, & 22, Year 1988

Ignorance under the Name of Islam

It is ridiculous that Mullahs cause people to be deprived of knowledge under the name of religion though Islam is the religion which has obliged both men and women to seek knowledge. But, we are unfortunate to be deprived of knowledge under the name of Islam.

Instructions and Articles of Bacha Khan, Page 10

Revenge

Our battle is based on patience; we don't take revenge of beating and abuse. We will be patient, submitting ourselves to God.
We are servants of God, so he will take our revenge.
Eradicate selfishness and dissension form your hearts because they have ruined us. Develop good ethics in yourselves because nobody can improve without good ethics.

My Life and Struggle, Page 536

Patience

Our struggle is based on nonviolence, and we will cope with any kind of hardship and disaster with patience. We will not take revenge as we are the servants of God who will take our revenge from the cruel.

Instructions and Articles of Bacha Khan, Page 19

Fear

I don't know why you are afraid of the English as they are also human beings and a nation like you.

You are vitiated due to being divided into parties and dissension which caused fear among you.

One who is afraid of God has no fear in heart and is afraid of no one else.

On the other hand, someone whose heart is not filled with fear of God is afraid of everyone.

Oh brothers, fill your hearts with fear of God!

My Life and Struggle, Page 536

Hidden Activity

The activity which someone cannot publicly does and tries to do it secretly leads to the person's weakness, prevents him from being in the framework of principles, creates fear in him, and makes him less confident.

The more someone decreases his ambitions and desires, the more he will be relaxed and pleased.

Instructions and Articles of Bacha Khan, Page 14

Criticizing Others

We are not here to raise objections or criticize others.
It is not up to us to criticize or blame other associations and their leaders.
We are here to present our own program to the people regarding what we want for them and that this task can't be accomplished alone. It will be possible when you accompany us. This country is shared by you and us; thus, as we share the nation, we should cooperate.

My Life and Struggle, Page 651

A Movement from Village

It was a movement for serving the creatures of God and humanity.
It had created enthusiasm in Muslims, Hindus and Sikhs, while there had been no predecessor of it.
It was a movement from village with its center in the village because most people of the nation reside in villages.
The difference of this movement from other movements is that others start from cities and spread into villages, while this movement initiated from villages and promoted in cities.

My Life and Struggle, Page 729

To the Indian Ambassador in Kabul

Afghans and Pashtoons will never accept communism or Russia. They will be killed, and if possible, some of them will leave their country.

I have to talk to Brezhnev; I will tell him "do a favor".

I will also tell Reagan "do a favor".

Communists in Afghanistan not only kill people but also destroy trees.

The revolution has turned into cruelty.

Ambassador! You are a youth; you should understand a catastrophe. There is a catastrophe going on in Afghanistan as Mujahidin kill people at nights while Soviet soldiers do so during the days.

As a result, Pashtoons are being killed.

An Afghan Diary: Zahir Shah to Taliban by Dixit, Page 30

Taking Care of Others

We always think of ourselves but don't take care of others. It is a big shortcoming; we need to always think of hardship and welfare of the God's creatures.

Instructions and Articles of Bacha Khan, Page 15

Letter of Bacha Khan to Noor Mohammad Taraki

To: Noor Mohammad Taraki

Offering respect, prays, greeting, good wishes and salutation,

When Lennon started revolution in Russia, he invited his party's leaders, governmental ministers and authorities in the first days. He gathered them and said to them that previously there used to be a King, and the governmental system was kingdom which treated the public unfairly; thus, people collapsed it and fulminated against it. As the people now are happy with our rule, we need to learn lessons from the previous situation.

We should treat people in a proper manner, serve them and keep them happy so that in return they will always support us.

Beware that we should not commit any sort of poor treatment and cruelty due to which people will miss the past kings; otherwise, it will be a big unfortunate for both ourselves and the country.

So, dear Taraki,

Invite your party's leaders and senior governmental officials and advise them to be mindful not to commit any improper actions, oppression or injustice, otherwise you will regret it, and people will also miss the previous kings and kingdom system…

Overview of the Thoughts and Historical Struggles of Khan Abdul Ghaffar Khan (Bacha Khan), Pages 84-85

Letter of Badshah Khan to Babrak Karmal

To: Babrak Karmal

Dear Babrak Karmal, I wish you a long life, right path, good health and happiness.

You are now not the Karmal I had met. You would love and feel sympathetic to the country, but now look at your country and the nation whether they have flourished or failed. Any country of the world where revolution occurred or Communism emerged, it has flourished, while we are destroyed due to it. Revolution is about change. This is neither revolution nor Communism; it is a conflict between two parties. One is backed by the USA and the other is supported by Russia. As a result, it is we who are vitiated by both sides. You need to contemplate the issue and find a solution for it, consulting your party and the nation so that there will be security in the country. It will bring about honor for you and will pave the way for security and improvement of the nation. If you reject what I said, by the passage of time, you will regret it.

Overview of the Thoughts and Historical Struggles of Khan Abdul Ghaffar Khan (Bacha Khan), Pages 86-87

Baby Scorpion

May God not give Pashtoons the power of doing wrong, or as baby scorpions, they will bite their own mom.

Success requires social movement and sacrifice.

Nobody understands the reality of sin and reward because of the ignorant scholars.

Instructions and Articles of Bacha Khan, Page 10

Message to Indira Gandhi

I clearly explained to you that all Afghans oppose communists.
I have also said to you that communism can never become dominant in Afghanistan. If the conflict continues, Afghans will be losing their lives.
You are the daughter of Nehru and have lived with Gandhi and his partners. You are as my daughter too.
In Afghanistan, children, women and men are killed.
Don't you have some mercy in your heart?
An Afghan Diary: Zahir Shah to Taliban by Dixit, Page 93

Ghaffar Khan: Non-violent Badshah of the Pakhtuns by R. Gandhi, Pages 255 & 256

Friendship with Evil People

There is no need for being friends with evil, immoral people, even if they are brothers because they harm the nation and society and vitiate the people.

As currently Pashtoons follow wrong paths, it is because we do not differentiate between good and bad, and there is no one to guide us in this respect.

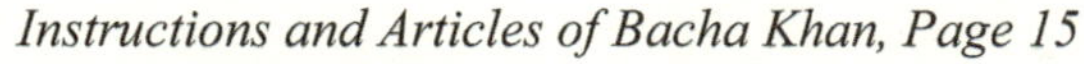
Instructions and Articles of Bacha Khan, Page 15

Religion and Heart

Islam did not come to our country in the way of religion. It came in the manner of politics, seizure of territories, force, and violence.

There is no need for force in religion, rather, it is opposite to force.

"There is no compulsion in religion." Religion belongs to heart, and heart does not accept something with force; it accepts things with knowledge. So, religion is not spread by force, but by preaching.

Letters of Bacha Khan, Volume II, Page 72

Inessential Expenses

This is a big unfortunate and ignorance of ours (Pashtoons) that we spend thousands of Rupees for rituals, but we are not willing to pay a single penny for the welfare of the nation, country and society.

Instructions and Articles of Bacha Khan, Page 9

Revolution

Revolution is not about hurry, nor is it easy. It is to be carried out with patience. It needs knowledge and wisdom. It also needs scholars and knowledgeable people who should educate the nation to get ready for revolution.

Revolution is like a sudden flood that moves those who are sleeping, while those who are awake take its advantages.

Revolutionary reforms can adjust the society however these reforms require revolutionary mindset and determination.

Instructions and Articles of Bacha Khan, Page 10

Violence and Nonviolence

The weapon of violence is gun.
Nonviolence is about spreading love among people as well as encouraging patience, aspiration and bravery.
Violence creates hatred, fear and anger as you can consider it in the people's lives before Islam in Mecca where there was violence.
However, all the well-known Islamic companions who did great practices were from Mecca, being the followers of nonviolence.

Letters of Bacha Khan, Volume II, Page 72

Bacha Khan: Please contemplate my sayings that violence cause hatred, but nonviolence leads to love.

Pashtoons use violence against their own brothers in their own home; thus, damaging themselves.

Honorable Memories of the Great Servant of God, Page 59

Patience

Nonviolence is basically a power as violence is. It also has army as violence does. However, the weapon of nonviolence is to preach, but that of violence is a gun. Nonviolence creates love, courage and confidence among people, but violence causes hatred, fear and timidity. Some argue that we need violence for the purpose of defense, but they don't feel that we can't practice nonviolence if we use violence for defense.
However, nonviolence itself is the defense. It does not collapse, but violence does. The same as there is a system for violence, nonviolence has a perfect system. Violence is easy, and following it is easy too, while non-violence is the opposite of the case; it is easy to react to a slap with a slap, but to tolerate one's slap is hard.

Rubies and Pearls, Page 30

Muslims

Muslims have forgotten Islam, and that is why one brother is enemy of another.

Instructions and Articles of Bacha Khan, Page 21

Education and Training of Girls

Day by day, my attention tends more towards the education and training of girls because I consider it hazardous for the nation to educate only boys and deprive girls of it.

As a result, our boys at first will not be willing to get married to uneducated girls, yet if they do, there will often be disorder and arguments in their households. It is a concern that this will cause a big damage to our country and the nation.

Letters of Bacha Khan, Volume I, Page 15

Independent Government

The Frontier province is the property of Pashtoons, so it should be governed by them too.

Honorable Memories of the Great Servant of God, Page 28

Disagreement

There is always disagreement among people which is just fine.

The Prophet (peace be upon him) has called disagreement a blessing. However, it is currently a trouble among Muslims especially Pashtoons.

Our disagreements often result in selfishness which has always harmed Pashtoons throughout their history.

Letters of Bacha Khan, Volume I, Page 56

Ethical Courage

To leave a tradition is very difficult, but it needs ethical courage.

Incorrect propaganda needs to be dealt with as one should stand firmly to make the people understand the truth. It is possible when there is a group of selfless friends with the same opinions who are trusted by the people.

Instructions and Articles of Bacha Khan, Page 14

Guarding the Current World

Today's world can be safeguarded from the evil of nuclear weapons only with following the nonviolence.

The world needs people like Gandhi to spread the message of friendship, love and peace to more people, given that they really don't want the civilization and humanity wiped off from the earth's face.

Nonviolent Soldier of Islam by Eknath Easwaren, Page 7

Pray

Pray for me that may Allah grant me courage, power and health for the service.

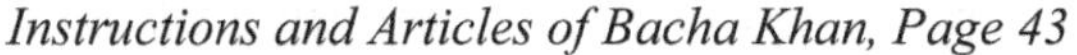

Instructions and Articles of Bacha Khan, Page 43

Oath of Service for God

- I am a servant of God. However, as God doesn't need to be served, serving His creatures is the same as to serve Him. I promise to serve the humanity for the sake of Allah.

- I promise to avoid violence as well as taking revenge.

- I promise to forgive those who are unfairly cruel to me.

- I promise to avoid rivalry, dispute and conflict and not to get involved in hostilities.

- I promise to treat any Pashtoon as my brother and friend.

- I promise not to violate the social customs, traditions, rites and order.

- I promise to live a simple life, follow goodness and avoid evil and bad activities.

- I promise to have fair behavior, temper and virtue. I promise not to be lazy and to dedicate at least two hours daily for social activities.

My Life and Struggle, Autobiography of Badshah Khan as Narrated to K.B. Narang, Page 97

Opportunist

It is not needed to have onlookers and those who are selfish and opportunist in the party. It needs investigations to include individuals who really want to join the party for the purpose of serving the nation, not being selfish.

Instructions and Articles of Bacha Khan, Page 20

Right and Republic

Imam Hussain stood for the right and republic, and we are here for the right and republic too. He was oppressed and so are we. He stood against cruelty, and we have stood for the same purpose.

Instructions and Articles of Bacha Khan, Page 11

Escaping from the Scene

Political prisoners need to take each step carefully and not to force others. If compelled people are able, they will escape from the field.

Rubies and Pearls, Page 44

Gardening

Hobby is allowed. Gardening is my favorite toil. I like it. I have been bestowed with a big piece of land.

Instructions and Articles of Bacha Khan, Page 31

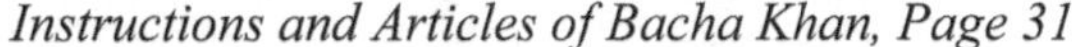

Know Yourself!

Know yourself!
Know your God!
And know your friend and enemy!
What else to write?
May Allah the Almighty grant us all patience and independence.
And may He give us the success and power to serve His creatures.

Letters of Bacha Khan, Volume I, Page 125

Mutual Visits

This is not service that I stay in my place while people come to visit me. I should go to visit them too.

Honorable Memories of the Great Servant of God, Page 73

Religion

It is an obligation of the followers of each religion to vanish hatred among the God's creatures, create love among them and help each other. But, has anyone informed us about this reality? There are religions among people, but just so-called religions. Religion encourages love, not hatred.

God will give us the power as He is the true owner of power.

I am happy to be in my country among my people, no matter if I am hungry and in trouble.

Neither Pakistan nor Islam matters, but the right of this nation of the poor people does.

What you don't wish for yourself, don't wish it for others either.

Also, if there is anyone misbehaving among us, the Pashtoons, his company should be avoided.

Instructions and Articles of Bacha Khan, Page 7

Word and Action

Ghani is an amazing boy, but he is not independent in temper. He talks much but acts little. Hopefully, he will be reformed with your attention.

Instructions and Articles of Bacha Khan, Page 47

To Eliminate the Cruel

Our duty is to eliminate cruelty from the world and protect the oppressed from the cruel, even if the cruel is our brother and Muslim.

Instructions of Bacha Khan, Page 4

Best of the Creatures

Human being is called to be the best of all the creatures of God; thus, his responsibility is higher than other creatures. However, as I see my people, I notice no difference between them and animals. They are concerned about filling their stomach, and so are the animals. They bear children and take care of them, and animals also bear their young and raise them. So, how could be called them the best of creatures? They kill each other like animals do.

They will be worth calling the best of creatures once there is social brotherhood, feeling of kinship, love and affection among them. Humans cannot be the best if the only difference is that other animals walk on four legs, but humans walk on two legs.

Instructions and Articles of Bacha Khan, Pages 12-13

Correction and Power

Such a brave and great nation does not have a national newspaper in its native language.

As per the history of the world, when some persons emerge among a nation for its correction, they are opposed by those who are in power because they felt it as a risk to their authority. Look at your own Khudai Khidmatgar movement; the more the nation has been informed, the more the powerful people's power has decreased.

Instructions and Articles of Bacha Khan, Page 13

Paying Tribute to Human

As a servant of God, I don't travel in rickshaw as it is driven by a human.

Rubies and Pearls, Page 14

Others vs. Us

Other nations of the world have become prosperous, developed and traveled to the skies while we are jealous of their lives and prosperity. They are humans like us, and were not born better than us. They found national sense, ethnical unity, respectfulness, knowledge, wisdom, love and affection; thus, they improved. We don't have such attributes; therefore, we have turned to dust.

Instructions and Articles of Bacha Khan, Page 14

To Blame Others or Oneself?

It is a big flaw of our people that we always try to unveil and find the weaknesses and defects of others while we don't give attention to our own weaknesses and defects. This is the cause that we are deprived and poor in today's world. Instead of criticizing others, we need to blame ourselves, and correcting ourselves is the first obligation before correcting others – first oneself then others.

Instructions and Articles of Bacha Khan, Page 15

Rules and Law

Where there is no justice, rules and law, and a person's word acts as the law, there will be no benefit of discussion with the person.

You can make others happy if you suffer hardship by yourself. If one cannot complete a work, he should not initiate that as it is better not to do it at all.

Instructions and Articles of Bacha Khan, Page 16

Youths' Work

Before starting any work, the youths need to think very much about it and contemplate its consequent hardship. If they are ready to bear all the hardship, then they may initiate the work. Otherwise if they cannot endure the hardship, it will be better to stay inside their houses and pray because such timidity of them harms the national goal.

Instructions and Articles of Bacha Khan, Page 16

Draw a Veil over Our Weakness

We can hide our weaknesses from people's sight, but we cannot hide them from God. So, what will be our response to Him? As we cannot hide our weaknesses from God, we don't need to hide them from people either; thus, we should frankly say what we can do and what we can't.

Instructions and Articles of Bacha Khan, Page 16

To Ghani

Translate other books too.

I congratulate you on publishing your articles in the newspapers.

Thanks to God that you succeeded in your intentions. Does this success encourage you or not?

Instructions and Articles of Bacha Khan, Page 65

Confidant

We should not hate anyone, rather we should fairly treat everyone. However, against your own group, do not become friend, confidant and supporter of anyone. We need to be confidant and supporters of our own company.

Instructions and Articles of Bacha Khan, Page 16

Not everyone should be informed about personal secrets and intentions.

Rubies and Pearls, Page 44

Effect of Speech

If someone's actions are contrary to their words, the speech will not have any effect on the people.

The surety among nations is based on believing and trusting each other.

Diplomacy is hypocrisy, and I am not hypocrite to say something but not believe it by heart.

Instructions and Articles of Bacha Khan, Page 17

Lie does not last long, and it disappears as soon as the truth emerges.

Instructions and Articles of Bacha Khan, Page 17

Freedom and Prosperity

Freedom is the means of a nation's prosperity. Freedom is easy, but prosperity is difficult. Prosperity can only be achieved through enthusiasm for service for the sake of God.
It is a big weakness of ours as Muslims that we don't investigate what we hear.

Instructions and Articles of Bacha Khan, Page 21

The plant of freedom grows by irrigating it with the blood of the youth.

Instructions and Articles of Bacha Khan, Page 17

Honor of Nations

As long as I am alive, I will be working in the country for achieving honor, republic and justice.

Pashtoon is strong for getting profit but not for solidarity.

If there is a conflict between cruel and oppressed, we will stand with the oppressed.

In big meetings, sessions and long speeches, the honor of nations is damaged.

Instructions and Articles of Bacha Khan, Page 22

Building Own Home

If you want to have yourselves freed, poverty alleviated, the naked covered and the hungry fed, then build your own home, avoid hostility and disunity, and differentiate between friend and enemy.

Uneducated people are easily deceived under the name of religion.

Crops are always grown from the seed which gets under the soil.

Those who are lacking civility cannot accomplish any work.

I am the preacher and speaker of sincerity and love.

Instructions and Articles of Bacha Khan, Page 23

Help Yourselves

The cause of poorness and misery of the Indian nations is that they don't work by themselves, rather they expect from others. Some of them say Imam will come, and others are waiting for Avatar. These unfortunate people don't know that even if the Imam and Avatar come, they will help those who help themselves.

Instructions and Articles of Bacha Khan, Page 30

Ahmadabad Prison

In Ahmadabad prison, I talked to you about the spinning wheel, and I also mentioned it to Mahadev Ji. Now, I have free time for spinning, so please send me my own or any other spinning wheel with its yarn.

Instructions and Articles of Bacha Khan, Page 32

Significance of Time

Humans are weak and make mistakes, so one should understand weakness and try to correct it. For doing so, there is no better and more appropriate place than a prison. Thus, we should let ourselves and our friends know not to waste our time by worthless talks, but to learn writing. In prison, there is an opportunity to learn something and acquire good ethics, fair behavior, patience and perseverance so that we will be able to serve the creatures of God for His sake as well as to create love and affection in our homes.

Instructions and Articles of Bacha Khan, Page 35

People Who Love the Nation

First, try to build your own home. If not, at least accept this suggestion of mine that do not oppose each other in the elections.
I believe that if there are people in a nation who are selfless and love the nation and movement, that nation and their country will flourish. May God create more such people in the nation.

Instructions and Articles of Bacha Khan, Page 39

May God grant you good health for service of the nation and country.

Instructions and Articles of Bacha Khan, Page 42

The Poor

This is a poor country and you are poor too. The parties and improper expenses are not consistent with your and the country's economy; think about yourselves and the country.

Honorable Memories of the Great Servant of God, Page 47

Goodness and Badness

The goodness or badness of each person belong to himself. If someone is good, it is his own advantage. And if someone is bad, he himself will be in trouble.

Borrowing money is a bad habit, and not trying to pay off the debt is worse than that.

I am released to tour around the world.

Give my greetings to Ms. Meem and tell her that I pray for her health.

Regard my love and affection to Maryam and Tajo and start teaching them Pashto writing and reading. Tell them and Ms. Meem that both of the girls are my children whom I will dedicate to serve the poor Pashtoons. I expect much from them; are they also ready to realize this hope of mine?

Instructions and Articles of Bacha Khan, Page 44

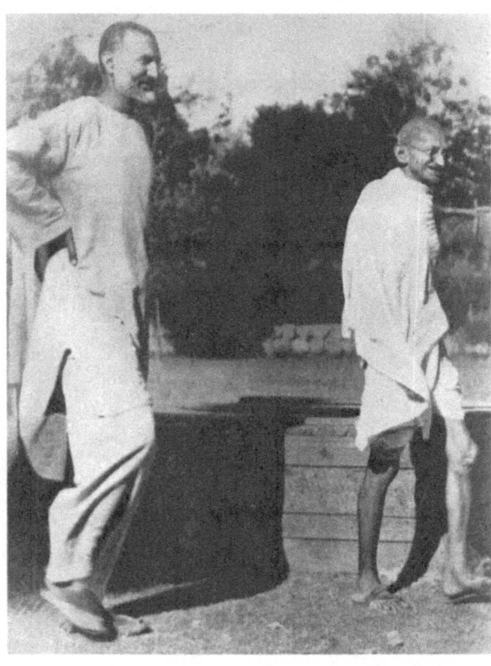

Good Vs Bad Person

Officials now need to achieve three types of trust. It can be achieved not with saying but practically with action. If others treat us badly, we should react with good actions. Otherwise, if we are bad against their bad actions, what will be the difference between us and them? We will then be as bad as they are.

A good person is the one who reacts with good manner against others' bad treatment; thus, he will be called a true servant of God. For reaching God, the means is to serve His creatures as His satisfaction is gained through the happiness of His creatures.

As an arrested person is upset, I will send him this pen. In today's circumstances, Pashtoons don't need guns, but they need pen because the freedom of our country will be realized with pens, not the guns.

Instructions and Articles of Bacha Khan, Pages 48-49

Useless Discussion

An opinion should be expressed once to the world. If it is accepted, that will be very good otherwise no extra discussion is needed because arguments have not been concluded.

Go once again to the workshop and receive enough qualification in the work. However, this time, pretend yourself as a student.

Instructions and Articles of Bacha Khan, Page 51

Purpose of the Movement

This movement was launched with the purpose to protect the oppressed from the cruel, no matter if the cruel is a Muslim, a Hindu or an English.

Rubies and Pearls, Page 14

To Wali Khan

I tell you that be very mindful of your health as well as your eyes.
Your meetings should always be with good people. Do good deeds; avoid contacting bad persons; and have control over yourself. As you are a child, it is not good to acquire the bad habit of prodigality as Ghani did.

Instructions and Articles of Bacha Khan, Page 52

I and Wali Khan are of the same opinions with the only difference that I am a reformist, spiritual man while he is a political leader.

Instructions and Articles of Bacha Khan, Page 22

Calculation

Testing for the second chance is foolishness. Write to Ghani to send me the sum of all money spent.
Don't give them more than forty Rupees per month, and their rent should be at a level lower than the others.

Instructions and Articles of Bacha Khan, Page 52

Misunderstanding

Do not provide him with cash as he doesn't know to properly spend the money. I get very upset when Ghani write me in letter that good people don't lie. However, I get quite happy that after hearing my advice, he didn't hide his feeling, but he wrote it down and sent me. Hopefully, he will always do the same in the future; not to hide his reaction to what he hears as hiding it can lead to much misunderstanding.

Instructions and Articles of Bacha Khan, Page 53

Keeping Promise

I will send you the list of my expenses each month, but you didn't keep your promise. This is not good because if one promises, he keeps his word. Work hard in your studies, don't be spendthrift, don't lie, don't borrow money from others, live on what is allocated to you.

Instructions and Articles of Bacha Khan, Page 54

Prosperity of Nation

For the rehabilitation and inspiration of nations, people are needed who are selfless, righteous, faithful and ready to serve their nation for the sake God. Once there are such individuals in a nation, their efforts will result in love, affection, sympathy, brotherhood and rapport among the people.

Thus, the nation reaches prosperity.

Instructions of Bacha Khan, Page 2

Our Duty

We are servants of God. We endure hardship for the benefit and welfare of others.

Our duty is service and beneficence no matter how people treat us, we do not try to take revenge.

Our obligation is to forgive and have patience.

Instructions of Bacha Khan, Page 3

To Serve God's Creatures

Though Khudai Khidmatgar call themselves the servants of God, God doesn't need to be served; to serve His creatures is like serving Him. God's creatures are not only Muslims, but all humans whether Hindus, Sikhs or Christians.

Instructions of Bacha Khan, Page 5

There is no room for opposition in service.

Instructions and Articles of Bacha Khan, Page 16

A Work for the Sake of God

We Pashtoons consider a work or service to be for the sake of God when it is done without any expectation, ulterior motive, or wage. God doesn't need to be served; to serve His creatures is as to have served Him.

We have started marches village by village and home by home for the purpose of public awareness and creating love, affection, brotherhood, and sense of national unity, encouraging enthusiasm for education, removing improper customs and traditions from the nation, and attracting donations for national schools; thus, it has resulted in inspiration and emotion for life among the public. These marches of ours, however, caused fear among the English.

For the sake of God and your oppressed nation, remove hatred and rancor from your hearts as these feelings have harmed and damaged us.

If you really would like your nations and country to be successful, then bury yourselves under soil as the seeds of wheat because unless a seed is buried, it can't grow.

Instructions of Bacha Khan, Pages 5, 6, 7, 8, & 9

To Bring about Change in People

The reality is that only the law can't reform a country and ensure security. To change the people's mindset is needed because unless the public mindset is changed, crimes can't be mitigated.

The people's mindset can only be changed by the movement of Khudai Khidmatgar. The more this movement spreads, the more the people's mindset will change, and its ultimate result will be security and safety in the country. No matter how good and courageous their members are, when there is opposition among parties, they become useless as their power will be consumed in defeating each other. In service, there is no space for opposition because opposition is rooted in selfishness. Whatever I like for myself, I like that for my companions too.

I often ask my friends that anytime you notice any drawback in my speeches, writings, conversations, manners or behaviors, please inform me about that. Whenever they let me know about my mistakes, I thank them and try to correct my shortcomings.

Violence leads to hatred, but non-violence results in love.

Human beings are strange creatures; when they get weak and lose courage, then they try to find various excuses and pretexts for hiding their weakness and discouragement.

Instructions of Bacha Khan, Pages 10, 11, 12, 13, & 14

Divine Religions

The truth is that all the divine religions are from God and are conveyed to the earth for unity, love, affection and the wellbeing and service of God's creatures.

It is the obligation of the followers of each religion to eliminate hatred and rancor and to create love and affection among the people as well as to help each other. But, no one has informed us about this truth.

Instructions of Bacha Khan, Page 15

Service of Country and Religion

Service of country and religion can be done by the one who first corrects himself, reforms his morality, and knows his principles. The one who doesn't know his principles and has bad behaviors cannot benefit other creatures of God.

Rubies and Pearls, Page 19

The Language of Amanullah Khan

One day, I met Amanullah Khan. I talked with him very much and told him: you can speak Turkish, Persian and other languages, but you can't speak your native language.

My words inspired him too much, making him promise that he will learn the language.

After he was expelled from Afghanistan, I went to Mumbai to meet him. There, he talked to me in Pashto.

Instructions of Bacha Khan, Page 23

Attention to Language

Whenever I talked with educated people about language, they would tell me "Pashto is not a proper language as there is nothing about science in it".

I told them, friends, other languages were not sent down from the sky either. It is the speakers of each language who improved their languages.

Since Pashtoons have not given attention to their language, what is the failure of Pashto in it? It is the fault of mine and yours.

The nation who underestimate their language will be disrespected, and those who lose their language will lose themselves.

One who forgets his language will become stranger from his relatives.

Instructions of Bacha Khan, Pages 24-25

Revolution

Revolution is not about hurry and ease.
Revolution is carried out with patience.
Revolution requires education and knowledge.
Revolution needs scholars and knowledgeable people who train nations with education to prepare them for revolution.
Revolution needs people.
Kingdom is something useless which is harmful for the nation and country.
If there is a good king today, his son will accede to the power tomorrow. So, who can guarantee that the son will also be good? Also, kings do not want their nation to improve because they assume that if the public improves, they will be discharged; therefore, they always prevent the nation to get educated.
We don't want to have kings; we don't need kings. We will have a leader elected with the nation's votes, will, and consultation. The leader will be the one who is servant of the nation.
He will not differentiate among the rich, poor, master or Mullahs, being someone who is righteous, faithful and sincere to the nation and country. He will be the one who has served the nation and country and has suffered hardship and sacrifice in this regard. Then, he will be qualified for the leadership. Our government will be dependent upon the community, not the opposite.
Pashtoonkhwa is the land of all Pashtoons, so we don't want one person to be the Khan. Rather, we will be trying to have all people rich. Also, we will establish a government in which there will be equality to be beneficial for all alike.

Whether it is more or less, it will be shared, having ensured security and justice. We will have a national Jirga authorized to select a leader.
Pashtoons, for the sake of God!
Be united!
Construct your home.
Avoid being divided into parties and groups with rivalries; thus, you will be successful in the hereafter as well as prosperous and peaceful in this world too.
There is no room for opposition in service as opposition is the child of selfishness.

Instructions of Bacha Khan, Pages 26, 27, 28, 29, 30, & 31

Unfair Traditions

My aim is not to oppose the government. I would like to reform Pashtoons so that they will avoid unfair traditions, bad customs, disunity, and division.

Rubies and Pearls, Page 14

Sacrifice

Unless the love and enthusiasm for sacrifice in a nation are strengthened to the maximum extent, the success of the nation cannot be envisioned.

I, to all of you, recommend the love and enthusiasm of sacrifice for improvement of the country and nation because as long as there is the power of sacrifice among us, nobody can defeat our Pashtoon nation. Also, I believe that the same as the English, eventually the government of Pakistan will realize that this land belongs to Pashtoons, so it should be governed by themselves.

Honorable Memories of the Great Servant of God, Page 30

Test

Today, the Pashtoon nation is put to the test. It is worth being thankful for that the nation is standing as strong as a mountain in this test.

Whether you want to change yourselves or not, the time has changed without considering anyone. Thus, I recommend to you the love and unity over enmity and rivalry, telling you that:

Gather around the identity of "Pashtoon" instead of Muslim League, Awami League, Islam League or Khudai Khidmatgar.

Honorable Memories of the Great Servant of God, Page 31

Arrest

I am not afraid of getting arrested, that is why I say the truth to the government. Those who are afraid cannot say the truth in front of the government.

Rubies and Pearls, Page 14

Pain of Country

Bacha Khan: Son, when your lords here get headache, they travel to London for treatment.

It is amazing, I come for treatment to Kabul from London.

Yes! My sickness is different. It is the pain of the nation and country. I hope I will find its treatment here.

Honorable Memories of the Great Servant of God, Page 48

Your Service

Bacha Khan: I am physically sick too.
Throughout the 23 years of Paskistan government, eighteen years of my age has passed in prison. It has made me too tired. I will rest here for a while, meet you dear brothers, and talk to you about brotherhood and relativeness.
There, I have served the people throughout my entire live, and as you are also my relatives, it is your right to serve you from now on.

Honorable Memories of the Great Servant of God, Page 49

Sincere Nation

Pashtoon nation is not to be blamed much as these poor people are humble and sincere. They love their leaders, but whoever has emerged under the name of their leadership, they have misused the humbleness and sincerity of this poor nation. Then, after the so-called leaders have reached their purposes, they have left the nation in poverty and hopelessness. No one has truly benefited the nation nor have they guided them to the right path of life.

Service of God, Page 10

A Servant of God

You people call me Baba (i.e. Grandpa). It is so kind of you, but I am not your Baba because your ancestors have destroyed you. I am your servant; I am a servant of God.

A servant of God is someone who serves God' creatures for the sake of Him, without expecting any pension, wage, money or remuneration. God doesn't need to be served; to serve His creatures is as to serve Him.

Look at the people of the rest of the world. To which extent have they improved by education and hard work? And what about us? We receive maize as donation from the USA, but that is also bitter.
Allah the Almighty has granted us a country like paradise, but we have turned it into hell due to ignorance, laziness, disunity, and rivalries.
We are hungry, thirsty, naked, and poor; but how long more?

Honorable Memories of the Great Servant of God, Page 70

As a servant of God, I consider it a sin to hate God's creatures. And to serve His creatures is as to serve Him.

Rubies and Pearls, Page 14

Hardship

Those who have stood to serve the creatures of God have suffered hardship and troubles.

Rubies and Pearls, Page 13

Nations of Words Vs Nations of Action

Nations of the world cannot improve only through ideas. The nations who talk much are as poor as us, and those who work instead of only talking are prosperous.
Other nations around the world are also like us, but they have reached the skies.
Pashtoons even cannot talk. The nation which cannot tolerate others' opinions, they cannot improve in this world.

Honorable Memories of the Great Servant of God, Page 83

The Difference Between Good and Bad

If a bad person considers that he is supported in his misbehaving, he will not end his bad actions. If we differentiate between good and bad and keep the promise that we make with God in each night prayer (i.e. و نخلع و نترک من یفجرک) that we will break ties with those who disobey you, then we Pashtoons will completely change. Thus, we should inform each Pashtoon about this and spread this message to each of them.

Rubies and Pearls, Page 16

Traditional Parties

Our Pashtoon brothers spend hundreds of Rupees on traditional parties, but they don't donate a single penny to the fundamental fund of nation. This is a cause that we are more backward than any other nation around the world.

Rubies and Pearls, Page 17

Influential People

A nation will accept to be influenced only when influential people emerge among them.

Rubies and Pearls, Page 25

Two Sayings of Khushal Khan

They talk much about Khushal Khan, but I recommend you to act upon two sayings of him:
First, avoid being attached to the world, and second, avoid love of personal power!
We are harmed by these attributes of us. If you look through the history of Islam, you will notice that treasures of Muslims became full and they seized East and West. But, when love of property and love and enthusiasm of personal power came into existence among Muslims, it resulted in disunity, domestic conflicts, and destruction.
So, if you exercise the two pieces of advice of Khushal Khan, you as well as your country will get rid of the poverty, wretchedness and destruction. I am not opposite to one's being rich and powerful as these are too crucial elements for a nation. You should get rich, given that your poor nation has a share in that.
I want authority and government, but not for being the director. If I like property and power, I like those to be used for service of the nation and country.

Honorable Memories of the Great Servant of God, Page 84

Own Land

Any land given to a nation by God is governed by themselves. The unfortunate is only in our case that the land belongs to us, but others take its advantages. We all should cooperatively work to free our country so that we as well as the generations to come will be prosperous.

Rubies and Pearls, Page 13

The Secret of Success

We all are Pashtoons, being a single nation, brothers of each other, and children of one ancestor; thus, our dignity and ignominy are shared. Accordingly, if we exercise the Hadith of Prophet Mohammad (peace be upon him) "i.e. what you don't like for yourself, don't wish it for others either", we will soon succeed.

Rubies and Pearls, Page 13

We need to reform our traditions and customs.

Rubies and Pearls, Page 25

Beneficial Opinion

This is a very beneficial notion for the nation and country to agree upon one person to lead them towards their overall goal. However, it should be considered that whether what the person does is for his personal profit or the nation's interest, and whether he works as per his own will or consult with colleagues. If his activities are for himself based on his personal decisions, he should not be followed as this position is achieved not through opposition but through service.

Rubies and Pearls, Page 14

Hypocrite

Our movement is founded on truth. We are not hypocrites to express one thing but believe otherwise.

Rubies and Pearls, Page 14

Diplomacy is hypocrisy, and I am not hypocrite.

Rubies and Pearls, Page 14

Nationalism

We are all Pashtoons after all, no matter to be Shia or Sunni. We are a single nation in one country, believing in the same God, following the same Prophet and having the same book the Quran. You accept Imam Ali (may God be pleased with him), and we accept him too. Then, what is the opposition for? If our paths are different, after all, we live in the same country. To serve this country is our mutual obligation.

Rubies and Pearls, Page 14

Our Mullahs

This is not based on Islam since Islam has obliged education on each Muslim man and woman. Our Mullahs don't give attention to worldly sciences and politics as well as our rich people don't care about religious education; hence, we are poor in this world and will be poor in the hereafter too.

Rubies and Pearls, Page 17

Shepherd

The poor Pashtoons are a good crowd of sheep, but they don't have shepherd. This crowd gathers around anyone, hoping him to be their shepherd and will protect them from wolves. However, when they line around him, he draws his knife form the sheath and slaughters them.

Rubies and Pearls, Page 18

Native Language

Though Pashtoons form a brave nation, they are very weak in respect to their language. Wherever they go, they forget their language and always embrace other language with the cost of losing their own language. I recommend you to teach Pashto to your children and try to have your letters and books written in Pashto. It does not mean not to learn other languages at all. Do learn other languages, given that you maintain your native language Pashto.

Rubies and Pearls, Page 18

For God Sake

Pashtoons, for the sake of God, construct your home, raise your voice cooperatively, mitigate domestic hostilities, avoid following past rivalries, do not testify unjustifiably, consider each other as brothers, and regard relativeness.

Rubies and Pearls, Page 18

Blood of the Nation

The plant of national freedom grows with the blood of the nation. Once it matures, the descendants of the scarified youth will rest under the shadow of the tree.

Rubies and Pearls, Page 18

Great Patience

The purpose for which we have exerted efforts and come to the scene requires a great deal of patience, endurance and tolerance.

Rubies and Pearls, Page 18

Confrontation with the Right

If the movement of Khudai Khidmatgar truly attempts to accomplish its duties, all can be reformed, resulting in brightening the darkness. The wrong cannot confront the right.

Rubies and Pearls, Page 19

Separate Branches

Pashtoons are a single nation. Whether they are Momand, Khalil, Yousufzai, Mohammadzai, Khattak, Bangash, Wazir, Masoud, Marwat, Bitani, Khalji or Shinwari, after all they are Pashtoons as separate branches of the same root.

Rubies and Pearls, Page 19

Assistance

My brothers! If you somewhat wish to improve your wretched life, then become true servants of God and put selfishness aside so that God will assist us in reaching our goals. Otherwise, if

we are looking for personal interests under the name of nation, remember that God will never help such a wretched nation.

Rubies and Pearls, Page 19

Service of the Nation and Country

Sisters! Service of the nation and country is not the obligation of men only, but it is your duty too.

Rubies and Pearls, Page 19

Simple Domestic Clothing

My sisters and moms! If you bear wearing simple domestic clothing, it will very much benefit your men as they will get rid of debts and will live with honor. This will be your service for the country as well. Moreover, if you daily in free times stitch as much thread to be enough for your and your men's clothing, believe that you will get rid of many expenses.

Rubies and Pearls, Page 20

Oppression and Cruelty

Our task is to tolerate oppression and cruelty. Thus, if one cannot bear it, he should not join the movement of Khudai Khidmatgar.

Rubies and Pearls, Page 20

Lie

The lie can really cause misunderstanding for some time among people, but it cannot resist when the truth is revealed.

Rubies and Pearls, Page 46

If someone believes one way but says otherwise, he does not have much influence over people.

Rubies and Pearls, Page 46

Trial

Oh Pashtoon brothers! Don't be hopeless because it is a trial of God on us in which we need to be careful. So, rise and serve the creatures.

Rubies and Pearls, Page 20

Causes of Devastation

Our struggle is based on patience, so we will be patient, leaving everything else to the Exalted Allah. We shall clear our hearts of dissension and eliminate selfishness because these are the causes of our devastation.

Rubies and Pearls, Page 20

Work in Public

The work which cannot be done in public creates fear and weakness in the doer.

Rubies and Pearls, Page 20

Enforcing the Law

If a good law is established with unfair intention, its enforcement will definitely be bad.

Rubies and Pearls, Page 21

Difficult Decisions

Troublesome and difficult decisions can never be made with a majority vote.

Rubies and Pearls, Page 21

Movements

One of the differences between an individual movement and communal movement is that governments can prevent and wipe off individual's movements. This is the reason there is fear in individualistic behavior. On the other hand, governments cannot stop communal movements because in such joint efforts, there is no space for fear. Many individualistic movements headed by very strong Pashtoon leaders were eliminated by Moghuls, English and the government of Pakistan. However, as the Khudai Khidmatgar is a shared movement, it was neither stopped by the English oppressions, beatings, violence, imprisonments, disgrace, and tricks nor could it be dissolved by the Pakistan government's thirty-two years of cruelty, humiliation, murders, seizure of properties, detentions, permits and greed.

Rubies and Pearls, Page 22

Social Life

There used to be great kings and leaders of Pashtoons, but none of them created social life or the idea of social life among Pashtoons. Khudai Khidmatgar is the first movement that created social life and thoughts among them.

Rubies and Pearls, Page 23

The main reason behind Pashtoon's devastation and wretchedness is that no one has tried to bring about social life among them. Also, if you go through the history of Pashtoons, it has been ages that no movement has been initiated to be based on brotherhood, affiliation, love, affection and unity.

Service of God, Page 9

Religious Teacher

The poor Mullahs are not to be blamed. It is the nation's fault that we don't care about education and training of those [religious students] whom we are to fully authorize about the religion and sect. They ask for food home by home. For such a big duty, we train our religious teachers in such an awkward way. This is our own failure. The reality is that after we embraced Islam, we didn't quit some of the traditions and costumes from the times of being Hindus. The same as Hindus used to select various groups for different aspects of life, we continued to do the same. This is because Islam did not come here in the way of religion (i.e. through preaching), but it came by political manner (i.e. through swords). Thus, no one informed us about the reality of the religion, and we are still not aware of that. These are the traditional effects of the system of Kast that one group will be doing trade and other will be providing public service. This is not based on Islam since Islam has obliged education on each Muslim man woman. Our

Mullahs don't give attention to worldly sciences and politics as well as our rich people don't care about religious education; hence, we are poor in this world and will be poor in the hereafter too.

Rubies and Pearls, Page 24

Mutual Goal

Among those who has the same goal, there is always love and affection. Though there might be disagreement of opinions, it is a blessing for the group. As you witness the divisions in groups, if you study them, you will realize that they don't have mutual goal. Thus, the disagreement of opinions among them is a trouble rather than a blessing. It is because they don't work for God and His creatures, but for their personal interests.

Rubies and Pearls, Page 25

Educated

The love and service for nation and sense of freedom are not only in education. When we were to initiate the movement for service of the nation and freedom, I looked for educated people in cities, but I could not find who were ready for service of the nation for the sake of God.

Rubies and Pearls, Page 25

Usurper Governments

Usurper governments relies on creating fears among the public because once there is no fear among them, the foundation of such a government will be collapsed. A usurper government is like a theft who cannot stay when the house owner is awake.

Rubies and Pearls, Page 26

High Vs Low

Being morally high or low is based on actions. Regardless of being man or woman, if one's action is abhorrent, it should be considered low. In contrast, if one's action is great, it should be honored, no matter the person is a man or woman. God has created man and woman as two partners for the world's reclamation. They are like two wheels of the buggy of humanity which cannot move with one wheel. Especially Our Pashtoon women are so pious, modest and loyal, besides being ready to serve.

Rubies and Pearls, Page 26

Ruined Home

We have thoroughly realized the reason that English governed us is that their home is developed, and they are brotherly united. And, we are enslaved because our home is ruined.

Rubies and Pearls, Page 19

Embracing Religion

Those who are given a religion and have embraced and practiced it, they are prosperous in the world, possess dignity, have their own governments, and live in happiness and peace. Look at the Arabs. How was their status before Islam? And how did it improve after emergence of Islam and their practicing it? With Islam, they became the owners of government, property and prestige. Look at and think about each aspect of the lives of Muslims during the old times, then compare it what today's 'contractors of Islam' say regarding Islam. Is what they illustrate the Islam of God and the Prophet or the Islam based on the will of the rich? And is what they say for the sake of God or the rich?

Rubies and Pearls, Page 26

The Paradise-like Country

The history of Pashtoons is full of the narratives that whenever they had a chance, they authorized a master or Mullah over themselves instead of empowering their own brothers or relatives. They didn't like dignity for each other, and they didn't have goodwill for each other. Accordingly, those whom they accepted as the leaders of their country, nation or religion harmed and damaged them. Yet, they didn't learn lessons from it. This is why in this paradise-like country, they are even not full with maize and are hungry, thirsty, poor and ignorant.

They are deprived of the hidden resources that the Almighty has granted to their country. This situation will continue unless they change their tribal life into national life, become a united nation, create brotherhood, affiliation, national unity, love, affection and goodwill among themselves, and consider the honor of nation as their own honor as well the disrespect for the nation as their own disrespect.

Rubies and Pearls, Page 27

Political Interest

It is a propaganda that English were just. I accept they were just, but justice didn't matter in the issues which didn't have profit for them or where they otherwise had any political interest. Since they didn't recognize justice in political deals, in this case, they were crueler than any cruel you know.

Rubies and Pearls, Page 28

Religion of the Rich

Any religion or profession that comes under the control of selfish, tricky people, it will not preserve its initial revolutionary characteristics and nature. Then, it becomes a religion of the rich, being only in outline.

Rubies and Pearls, Page 28

Religious Wars

The Quran says that pious people believe both in the Quran and the other books sent by God. So, we don't know why and how wars under the name of religion started in the world.

Rubies and Pearls, Page 28

Soldier

As a soldier, I believe in deeds not in words.

Rubies and Pearls, Page 29

Slavery

In slavery, humans forget humanity, and humanistic attributes no longer exist.

Rubies and Pearls, Page 29

My Task

I am a servant of God, so my task is to serve all creatures of the Almighty Allah regardless of their origins or beliefs.

Rubies and Pearls, Page 29

Studying Religion

I am a religious person, so whatever I say or do shall be based on the religion. I recommend to both Muslims and Hindus to study their religious books because both of them act contrary to their religions. The religious books are not to be put on the shelves, but people should study and act upon their directions. As long as I know the Holy Quran and Gita, slavery is an execration according to them.

Rubies and Pearls, Page 29

Religion is Service

Religion is about love, morals and service for people. Religion is not for creating hatred among people, rather it is for wiping the hatred and rancor off the society. Disunity should not be brought about under the name of religion, and all of us should properly practice the teachings of our religion.

Rubies and Pearls, Page 29

Today's religion is for the luxury and revelry of a few, not for the welfare of God's creatures.

Instructions and Articles of Bacha Khan, Page 14

The reality is that today's religion is also controlled forcefully by the rich through their properties.
The true divine religion is about service of God's creatures, love, affection, justice, and fairness.

Instructions of Bacha Khan, Page 16

Feeling of Disgrace

We will not be united unless we understand that we are humiliated and disgraced.

Rubies and Pearls, Page 29

As human beings are mortal, I would say that when one definitely dies, it is better to die with honor and zeal.

Rubies and Pearls, Page 30

Being Proud of Culture

Slavery is an execration, yet people of India say they are blessed by God. Hindus say their culture is the most ancient culture throughout the world. Muslims are proud of the conquests of Shahabuddin Ghori and Mahmood Ghaznavi. However, Muslims are currently nothing, so there is no benefit of what they say that 'my father was a king'.

Rubies and Pearls, Page 30

Blessing and Torment

Slavery is a torment, and freedom is a blessing of Allah. If you consider the country to be yours, then the credit of what Hindus and Muslims do for the country does not belong to others. If you gain independence for your country, its advantage will be yours.

Rubies and Pearls, Page 30

Violent Ruler

Muslims are followers of the religion whose goal is to release the world from the chains of slavery. There is never any fear in the hearts of Muslims, so they are never afraid to say the truth in front of a violent ruler.

Rubies and Pearls, Page 30

Kings of the World

Mullahs have given the idea to people as if God is like kings of the world who require tax and gifts. They don't think about that God is in need of none and doesn't require anything nor anyone. Whatever of welfare, alms, charities, prayers, fasting, and Hajj are all for our own advantage. If you perform good deeds, it will not only help you succeed in this world, but it will also benefit you in the hereafter. On the other hand, if your actions are improper, you will be wretched, humiliated, and poor in the world, and you will be punished in the life after death.

Rubies and Pearls, Page 31

Experience

Instead of falling in moats to do new experiments or get experience, it is better to learn lessons from experience of those who have suffered much hardship and have fallen in various moats.

Rubies and Pearls, Page 33

Mullahs

Mullahs have caused many more damages to us. When any person, among us, have emerged for work and service, the Mullahs have either declared them as Wahabi or have stopped them from service by accusing them of being Hindu or non-believer. Neither they have served the people, nor have they let others do it. Without being helpful, they just offer prayers and eat food.

Rubies and Pearls, Page 31

Inheritance

According to Islam, to receive money against [marriage of] sisters or daughters is a big sin. Rather, Islam has defined their portion in the inheritance left from a father, mother or brother.

Rubies and Pearls, Page 32

Interest in Reading

Pashtoons are still not interested in reading newspapers. They spend thousands of Rupees for rituals, but do not pay a single penny to buy a newspaper. This is why, such a brave and great nation does not have a national newspaper.

Rubies and Pearls, Page 32

Fratricide

You Pashtoons are also like brothers in one home. As a non-believer does not kill another non-believer, you should not kill your Muslim brothers either.

Rubies and Pearls, Page 32

Stinginess

It is true that being stingy is a bad behavior however the generosity which makes one permanently indebted and needy is not good either.

Rubies and Pearls, Page 32

Destructive Criticism

Indeed, destructive criticism on people is an improper behavior because it doesn't have advantage. If one does not like to be negatively criticized, he should not like it for others. As one doesn't like something for himself, he should not like it for his other brothers.

Rubies and Pearls, Page 32

Determination

Whatever someone wants to do is possible, given that he has determination, patience and independence.

Rubies and Pearls, Page 33

The Reality of Sacrifice

No work in the world can be accomplished without suffering hardship and sacrifice. What is the reality of our sacrifice in comparison to the hardship and sacrifice that God's servants have suffered in the way of providing service to His creatures?

Rubies and Pearls, Page 33

Governance

Governance is about serving the nation, so it should be consistent with the nation's will and consent. If a government ignores the public consent, it will lead to disgrace instead of dignity.

Rubies and Pearls, Page 21

Children of Slaves

I don't disagree with marriage, but I don't like slaves to bear children. In today's conditions, I prefer [not to marry] if one has the tolerance.

Rubies and Pearls, Page 33

Routine Works

I daily work for four to five hours. I can work well with spade. I would like each member of Khudai Khidmatgar, regardless of being rich or poor, to daily work by themselves as work is full of blessings.

Rubies and Pearls, Page 33

Duty of Humans

The duty of humans is to work for correction, leaving its result to God as the result is known to Him.

Rubies and Pearls, Page 33

Close to Heart

Those who work for God without personal interest are close to my heart.

Rubies and Pearls, Page 33

Drinking Tea

I would like to let all members of Khudai Khidmatgar know that I consider the habit of unnecessarily drinking too much tea among Pashtoons to be dangerous for their future generations. However, the reason that I used to be quiet about this issue was that I myself drank tea. Therefore, I could not tell people in this regard because if one is not practicing his own advice, it will not have any effect on others. Now, I have quit drinking tea. It has been almost one year that I don't drink it. To quit any habit is difficult, but a firm determination and patience ease all the difficulty. For now, I request the members of Khudai Khidmatgar to drink tea once instead of two times daily or drink one cup of tea instead of two.

Rubies and Pearls, Pages 34

Superficiality

Each plan of Allah is for good, but we don't understand it because we consider it superficially. When we are seemingly somewhat in trouble, we get confused.

Rubies and Pearls, Page 36

Selfishness

Why are we and our country today in such a horrible situation? Why are we in this world such wretched and humiliated? The reason is that today each of us thinks and tries only for their personal improvement. There is selfishness; no matter if the

country or nation is damaged, but they should make profit. People are not ready for sacrifice and work; thus, Muslims are waiting for Imam, and the Hindus for Avatar. These are the signs of idle people that don't work for themselves and rely on others.

Rubies and Pearls, Page 35

Servant of People

Your dignity, happiness and success are my dignity, happiness and success. I am your servant who doesn't ask you any wage or remuneration for his service. I accomplish my obligation and ask the Almighty Allah for its reward.

Rubies and Pearls, Page 35

I get happy about your unity and improvement and get upset about your dissension and impoverishment. Day and night, I pray for your prosperity and freedom. May Allah enable us to serve His creatures.

Rubies and Pearls, Page 35

As before, I am still the servant of God. Whatever I do is for the sake of God and for the benefit and welfare of His creatures. I don't do it for any human to please him or receive any profit from him.

Rubies and Pearls, Page 36

Giving Foolish to Understand Something

To make a foolish person understand is easy and possible, but to make a wise person understand is impossible, let alone difficult.

Rubies and Pearls, Page 36

Dissension

I am so afraid of dissension because it has destroyed the home of Pashtoons.

Rubies and Pearls, Page 37

Authority

Unless Pashtoons have the authority over their own land, they cannot improve.

Rubies and Pearls, Page 37

We are to Succeed

As a servant of God, I believe that whatever is happening is for our good. We will eventually succeed, given that we stay firm to our principles and be true servants of God.

Rubies and Pearls, Page 37

Improper Issue

Argument is something improper, so it should be avoided as much as possible because its result is always unfair. Disagreement does exist, but it is enough to be expressed once. If it is accepted, it is fine, or else, there is no need to argue about that since arguments has never been concluded.

Rubies and Pearls, Page 37

National Service

Choose to live simply, and quit the habit of extra expenses as through doing so, national service is impossible.

Rubies and Pearls, Page 37

Denying a Mistake

If a person commits a mistake but does not admit it to be a mistake, his correction is difficult.

Rubies and Pearls, Page 37

Children of a Slave Nation

When children of a slave nation go somewhere, they don't acquire that community's good behavior, rather they bring its bad behavior with them.

Rubies and Pearls, Page 37

Domestic Clothing

My sisters, you know your country better that much property can be found here, but its government is controlled by others. Thus, as we are so poor as well as your brothers, fathers and husbands are in so pitiful situation, you should somehow be fair, meaning that to avoid wearing expensive foreign clothing such as 'Welayati' and Japanese fabrics. If you bear wearing simple domestic clothing, it will very much benefit your men as they will get rid of loan and live with honor.

Rubies and Pearls, Page 38

Means of Improvement

The means of nations' improvement differ from time to time. Previously those nations in the world were considered mighty who had physical power and could cause much bloodshed in battlefields, but today, a nation is regarded as powerful who has much power of pen, has means for propaganda, and publishes numerous newspapers and articles.

Rubies and Pearls, Page 38

Initiative

Our movement of Khudai Khidmatgar is not anything new; it is an ancient order from thirteen hundred and a half years ago, following the lifestyle of Prophet Mohammad (peace be upon him).

Rubies and Pearls, Page 39

Fond of Construction

Indeed, I am a person who is interested in construction, and I am by no means involved in destruction. Also, I believe more in action than in words. If you study my life, you will realize that I have dedicated all my life to the improvement and welfare of my country and nation.

Rubies and Pearls, Page 39

Ruin

I would like to repeat that I don't want Pakistan to be ruined. I don't want damage to anyone, Hindu, Muslim, Frontier Province, Punjab, Bengal, or Sindh. The benefit is in construction only. I frankly tell you that I will not support anyone in destruction. If you have any constructive objectives

and want to work in deed, not in words, for the country and nation, I declare in front of this honorable Iwan that my people will be ready to support you.

Rubies and Pearls, Page 39

Power and Force

Remember that power and force are not stable. You can temporarily use force, but if you keep forcing people, hatred against you will come into existence in their hearts. Don't do so.

Rubies and Pearls, Page 39

Tricks of the English

We need to avoid imitating the tricks and cheatings of English. If we keep following it, remember that we will lose the country we have gained with much hardship and difficulties.

Rubies and Pearls, Page 40

Trust

Most of the issues and problems are caused by mistrust. Such problems can be solved with trust. Governments are to be run with trust, not mistrust.

Rubies and Pearls, Page 40

Tolerance

Islam is a religion that teaches us about great deal of tolerance and patience. While exchanging ideas, we must very patiently treat each other. We should not oppose others for disagreeing with our ideas.

Rubies and Pearls, Page 40

Advantageous Activity

Consider Abu Bakr (may Allah be pleased with him) as a role model. Even before being appointed as the caliph, each of his activities was for the advantage of Muslims. As a caliph, he assigned himself as an ordinary member. Islam is blamed for inequality, but he practically proved that Islam believes in the equality of all humans' needs of life. No matter if a person is rich or poor, his requirements for life are the same. As all humans produce children, all of them have requirements. It is not like you assume that your requirements are more than ours. Also, you cannot say that there is no possibility for a poor to become rich reasoning that all facilities are only for the rich. These issues relate to culture and refinement where there should not be any difference [between the poor and rich]. Since physical requirements of all are the same, the same tasks should be assigned to all.

Rubies and Pearls, Page 41

Old Practices

I should like to tell you that our current behaviors and measures will never bring about happiness to us. We should quit the old practices and adapt to the methods of the first times

of Islam. We oppose this old system of government not only because it was given by the English, but as the main reason, because it does everything [wrong] under the name of Islam and we cannot allow doing so. If the government of Pakistan follows Islamic orders, I will definitely support it. My imagination for Pakistan is to be free. We want that there should not be only the rights for a certain group or certain individuals, but all its residents should have the same rights. Instead of a few individuals, all residents of the country should be subject to enjoying its freedom. We want the country to be governed by the public.

Rubies and Pearls, Page 41

Education in Native Language

It is quite difficult for a six or seven year old child to simultaneously learn a second language and get education; thus, the medium of instruction should be their native language.

Rubies and Pearls, Page 43

Dowry

Many people marry off their daughters against money. Family relationships should be based on humanity not to marry off a young girl to an old man against money.

Rubies and Pearls, Page 43

Brave Nations

A nation that lacks the feature of bravery and sacrifice delude themselves with the bravery and sacrifice of other nations.

Rubies and Pearls, Page 21

Educated People

I remember that when we started Pashtoon Magazine, I told the educated persons to take part in it and read it. They replied, what is there in Pashto? It is a dead language.

I told them Pashto is the same as other languages. Other languages were not sent down to be perfect form the sky either. Their educated speakers have worked for their languages. If there is nothing in Pashto means that there is nothing in you educated people. Whose fault is this? Pashto's or Pashtoons'?

Service of God, Page 4

Change

Yes! As you see the other successful nations of the world, the reason of their improvement is the people among them who have scarified their personal pleasure, comfort, prosperity and

improvement for the sake of their nation's and country's improvement, peace and prosperity. They have decayed themselves, but have flourished their homelands. The Quran also says that unless a nation change themselves, God will not change them.

Service of God, Page 9

Worry about Failure

Those are worried about failure who work for their personal aims while those who serve the creatures of God and work for the sake of God are not afraid to fail.

Rubies and Pearls, Page 21

Ruined Houses

O Pathans! Your house has fallen into ruin. Arise and Rebuild it – and remember to what nation you belong.

Nonviolent Soldier of Islam, Page 24

Our History

The history of my people is full of victories and tales of heroism, but there are drawbacks too. Internal feuds and personal jealousies have always snatched away the gains achieved through vast sacrifices. They were dispossessed only because of their own inherent defects, never by any outside power – for who could oppose them on the battlefield?

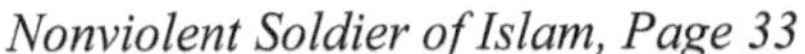

Nonviolent Soldier of Islam, Page 33

The Gateway of India

Our fault is that our province is the gateway of India. We were born in the Frontier province. This is why we were doomed and blamed.

Nonviolent Soldier of Islam, Page 45

The Real Muslim

The Prophet Mohammad came into this world and taught us: "A Muslim is who never hurts anyone by their word or deed, but who works for the benefit and happiness of God's creatures. Belief in God is to love one's fellows."

Nonviolent Soldier of Islam, Page 57

Islam!

It is my inmost conviction that Islam is work, faith, and love and without these the name "Muslim" is sounding brass and tinkling cymbal. The Quran makes it absolutely clear that faith in One God without a second, and good works, are enough to secure a man his Salvation.

Nonviolent Soldier of Islam, Page 64

Great Dream

I have one great dream and desire.

Like flowers in the desert, my people are born, bloom for a while with nobody to look after them, wither, and return to the dust they came from.

I want to see them share each other's sorrow and happiness. I want to see them work together as equal partners. I want to see them play their national role and take their rightful place among the nations of the world, for the service of God and humanity.

Nonviolent Soldier of Islam, Page 80

Hardship or Easy Life?

One learns good lessons from hardship. I wonder what would have happened to me if I had had an easy life, and had not had the privilege of tasting the joys of jail and all it means.

Nonviolent Soldier of Islam, Page 93

Love and Force

Is not the Pathan amenable to love and reason? He will go with you to hell if you can win his heart, but you cannot force him even go to heaven. Such is the power of love over the Pathans.

Nonviolent Soldier of Islam, Page 102

The Creed of Nonviolence

There is nothing surprising in a Muslim or a Pathan like me subscribing to the creed of nonviolence. It is not a new creed. It was followed fourteen hundred years ago by the Prophet all the time he was in Mecca, and it has since been followed by all those who wanted to throw off an oppressor's yoke. But we had so far forgotten it that when Gandhiji placed it before us, we thought he was sponsoring a novel creed.

Nonviolent Soldier of Islam, Page 111

The Weapon of the Prophet

I am going to give you such a weapon that the police and the army will not be able to stand against it. It is the weapon of the Prophet, but you are not aware of it. That weapon is patience and righteousness. No power on the earth can stand against it.

When you go back to your villages, tell you bretheren that there is an army of God and its weapon is patience. Ask your bretheren to join the army of God. Endure all hardships. If you exercise patience, victory will be yours.

Nonviolent Soldier of Islam, Page 127

Introduction

I have but one standard of measure and that is the measure of one's surrender to God.

Nonviolent Soldier of Islam, Page 145

Change of Life

As a young boy, I had had violent tendencies; the hot blood of the Pathans was in my veins. But in jail I had nothing to do except read the Koran. I read about the Prophet Mohammed in Mecca, about his patience, his suffering, his dedication. I had read it all before, as a child, but now I read it in the light of what I was hearing all around me about Gandhiji's struggle against the British Raj.... When I finally met Gandhiji, I learned all about his ideas of nonviolence and his Constructive Program. They changed my life forever.

Nonviolent Soldier of Islam, Page 157

Gandhi's Decision

Whenever Gandhiji takes an important decision, I instinctively say to myself, "This is the decision of one who has surrendered himself to God, and God never guideth ill."

Nonviolent Soldier of Islam, Page 168

Lessons of the Prophet

The Prophet faced many handicaps, but he never gave up hope, and finally triumphed. He has left that lesson behind, and if we face our difficulties in the same spirit, I do not see why we should ever fail. The cause of freedom is always just and the fight against slavery is always noble.

Nonviolent Soldier of Islam, Page 184

Struggle for Freedom

In my opinion, accepting slavery is a crime; therefore, unless there is the authority of the true people and equal, just opportunities are provided for all the residents of the country, I will continue my struggle for freedom, not accepting whoever ruling on us.

Nonviolent Soldier of Islam, Page 205

Hard or Easy Life?

I am grateful to God for the hardship in my early life. I don't know what would have happened to me if I had an easy life.

Ghaffar Khan: Nonviolent Badshah of the Pakhtuns, Rajmohan Gandhi, Page 68

Non-violence, A New Belief?

To be involved in non-violence for a Pashtoon or a Muslim is not strange. It is not a new belief.

Rather, it was applied around fourteen hundred years ago by the Prophet who always advised his followers to remove the burden of cruelty from the shoulders of humans.

But, we had forgotten this belief until Gandhi reminded us about that and supported this creed.

Khan Abdul Ghaffar Khan: The Apostle of Nonviolence, N Radhakrishnan, Page 1

Violence

You need non-violence before all because you commit violence against your brothers at your own home.

The Pride of Afghans and Afghanistan, Abdullah Bakhtani Khidmatgar, Page 93

The Reason of Our Destruction

Today's world has improved, but we have not. What is the reason of this? The reason is that today's world is for nationalism which we are lacking.

Historical Speeches of Khan Abdul Ghaffar Khan, Page 14

Revolution or Struggle?

Having witnessed the situation in Afghanistan and FATA, and after struggling in India, FATA and Afghanistan for fifteen years, I realized that revolution is not about hurry, nor is it easy. It is to be carried out with patience. It needs knowledge

and wisdom. Revolution also needs scholars and knowledgeable people who should educate the nation to get ready for it. Revolution needs people. Our emotional fellows enthusiastically emerged, but all of them dispersed later. Then, I thought to myself, concluding that our people do not give attention to either business, industry, agriculture or education.

On the other hand, they excessively follow customs and traditions and are busy with domestic conflicts. Such a nation cannot start a revolution, while they need to be freed from the disasters by inspiring them with political wisdom. To do so, a peaceful environment is required. Previously, I believed that all of these works need a revolution, and I perceived violence as a means of a successful revolution.

However, after the experience, I realized that horses cannot be trained during the battle. Therefore, I decided to return to my village and work based on the principles of non-violence.

My first decision was to establish national schools to educate and train the people for a revolution, so I came to Utmanzi. When I returned from migration, I tried to reactivate the schools closed by the English during the war.

Khudai Khidmatgar, Archiwal, Page 85

Need of the Nation

Non-violence has almost become my religion. I had already accepted this ideology, but after experiencing exceptional success in my province, I wholeheartedly embraced non-violence. The people of my province will never use violence, Insha'Allah.

However, it is possible that I will fail, and consequently a storm of violence will occur. If this happens, I will have patience with my fate. However, it will not bring about any change in my belief. Non-violence is good, and my nation needs it the most.

Freedom Movement and Bacha Khan by Farigh Bukhari, translated by Sajad Zhwandoon, Page 224

Pray

Oh God, remove the hatred, jealousy, detestation, hostility and animosity from the hearts of Pashtoons, and empower us to serve our nation and the country.

Oh God, destroy the enemies of Pashtoons, and empower us to distinguish between our friends and enemies.

Historical Speeches of Khan Abdul Ghaffar Khan, Page 10

Chronology

1889 Birth in the house of Bahram Khan in Utmanzai, Charsada

1897 Basic education in Masjid with Mullah

1898 Admission in Peshawar School

1998 Admission in Peshawar Municipality School

1906 Denying to join the English Army

1908 Aligarh Islamic School

1909 Decision not to travel to England for studying at college

1910 Inauguration of the first school in Utmanzai

1911 Joining the movement of Haji Sahib in Trangzai

1912 Marriage with Meher Qand (daughter of Yar Mohammad Khan)

1913 Participation in the conference of Muslim League in Agra

1913 Birth of the first son, Ghani Khan

1914 Fasting for 40 days together with the tribes in Bajawar

1915 Birth of the second son, Wali Khan, and death of wife

1919 Remarriage with Nambata daughter of Sultan Mohammad Khan

1919 Imprisonment for six months

1920 Release; another marriage, traveling to Delhi for attending Khilafat Conference, meeting with Gandhi, Abul

Kalam Azad and others; immigration with some others to Afghanistan for the issue of Khilafat, participation in session of Indian National Congress

1921 Establishment of a high school in Utmanzai called "Anjuman-Islah-e-Afghania" i.e. Afghan Reform Society; appointment of Abdul Akbar Khan as the society's first chairman; imprisonment for three years

1922 Birth of the second wife's daughter Mehertaj

1922 While being in prison, birth of the third son Abdul Ali Khan who later was the deputy chancellor of Peshawar University

1923 Appointment of his elder brother Khan Sahib as a doctor at Saint Thomas Hospital in London, who married an English women and then had a son Jan Khan and a daughter Maryam

1923 Death of mother

1924 Release; receiving the honorary title of 'Fakhr-e Afghan' i.e. Pride of Afghan; pilgrimage to Mecca for Hajj; visiting some Islamic countries; death and burial of wife in Jerusalem

1926 Death of father in whose funeral an unprecedented number of people participated; in the funeral ceremony, he asked the people, "I have dedicated 2000 Rupees as alms. Should I give it to the people or school?" People loudly said, to the school! To the school!

1927 Establishment of 'Anjuman-e Zamindaran' i.e. Society of Landowners, for the improvement of agriculture; creation of Pashoon Jirga 'Pashtoon Youth League' under his guidance

1928 Participation in meetings of Khilafat and Congress in Kolkata

1928 Pashtoon Magazine

1929 Establishment and foundation of Khudai Khidmatgar movement

Starting 'Pashtoon' publication; participation in Congress meeting in Lucknow of Lahore; meeting Gandhi and Nehru;

1930 Release from prison; starting visits to villages; participation in Congress meeting in Karachi; membership in the working committee of Congress with Gandhi; imprisonment with all members of congress

1931 25 August: Going to Simla with Gandhi and Jawaharlal Nehru to meet viceroy

1931 Making decision to inaugurate the congress branch in Peshawar

1931 Imprisonment for three years

1931 Pashtoon Magazine

1930 Massacre at Qisa Khwani Bazar in Peshawar

1931 His and other Khudai Khidmatgar members' release from Dera Ghazi Khan prison

1931 Traveling to Karachi with 100 members of Khudai Khidmatgar for congress meeting

1931 Going with Gandhi for a meeting of congress working committee

1931 July: arrival of Mahatma Gandhi's son Devdas Gandhi to Peshawar for examining the situation in frontier; he lived with Bacha Khan in Utmanzai.

1934 Release; expelled from Pashtoonkhwa; staying with Gandhi in Wardha; visiting Muslims in Bengal; rejecting to lead congress; speech in Mumbai; imprisonment

1934 17 August: Fasting for a week to accompany Gandhi's fasting

1934 30 September: speaking to a public gathering in Kolkata about unity of Hindus and Muslims

1935 Release; expelled from Pashtoonkhwa

1937 Expelled by Pashtoonkhwa governor; return to home; success by majority of vote in the provincial level; appointment of Khan Sahib as the governor

1938 Initiating construction program in Pashtoonkhwa

1938 1 May: Gandhi's visit to Frontier province for eight days

1940 Inaugurating a center for construction programs in Sardaryab; leaving congress for the reason of congress' getting distant from nonviolence

1941 Establishment of a training camp for members of Khudai Khidmatgar

1942 Civil resistance in Pashtoonkhwa

1942 Arrest by police while delivering speech; detention for two years; break of two of his ribs due to beating by police

1942 Gandhi and Bacha Khan's resignation from Indian National Congress and its working committee due to India's participation in the World War II.

1942 Establishment of 'High Center of Khudai Khidmatgar' in Sardaryab, 16 miles from Peshawar

1944 Imprisonment

1945 Release

1947 Asking members of Khudai Khidmatgar to boycott referendum; seizure of Pashtoon magazine by government of Pakistan in August

1947 Meeting of Khudai Khidmatgar for recognizing Pakistan, in September

1948 Oath of loyalty to Pakistan; elected leader of Pakistan People's Party; imprisonment along with Dr. Khan Sahib and the oppressed members of Khudai Khidmatgar, in June

1948 March: Pakistan People's Party establishment with G. M. Sayed, Abdul Majid Sindhi, Sheikh Hasamuddin and Abdul Samad Khan Achakzai also knows as 'Baloch Gandhi'; Bacha Khan was the first leader of this party.

1952 Death of Qazi Ataullah who was Bacha Khan's close friend and education minister when Dr. Khan Sahib was Chief Minister

1954 Release from prison; confinement in home; membership of Dr. Khan Sahib in Pakistan central cabinet

1955 Return to Pashtoonkhwa after seven years of imprisonment; election of General Iskandar Mirza as the president of Pakistan; declaration of a unit through which

frontier tribal areas (i.e. Pashtoonkhwa) was integrated as a unit of Pakistan

1956 Imprisonment, and seizure of all property of Bacha Khan's family

1957 Foundation of 'National Awami Party' in July; murder of Dr. Khan Sahib in May

1958 Arrest and detention, October

1959 Release from prison because of old age and sickness; inhibited from any kind of official job or governmental position

1961 Arrest and detention along with hundreds of his other colleagues

1962 Named as 'Prisoner of the Year' by Amnesty International;

1964 Release from prison; home confinement; allowed to travel to England for medical treatment; interview with Olaf Caroe writer of 'The Pathans' book; getting Afghan business visa in Cairo; traveling to Kabul; choosing to live in Kabul and traveling to different parts of Afghanistan.

1969: Traveling to India for speaking in Gandhi's 100th birthday anniversary; fasting for three days for the unity of Hindus and Muslims and praying for the welfare of the tribes

1971 Return to Pakhtoonkhwa after end of the twelve years old military government in Pakistan

1975 Imprisonment; National Awami Party banned; release from prison because of old age and continuous sickness

1983 Arrest with his son Wali Khan and other senior members of opposition; home confinement; end of confinement; visiting hospital for treatment;

1984 Hospitalization in Kabul

1985 Traveling to India with his son Wali Khan to participate in the 100th anniversary of the Indian National Congress

1987 Traveling to India for medical treatment as a guest of Indian government; honored with the highest civilian award of India called ‘Bharat Ratna’ (Jewel of India) as the first non-Indian; hospitalization in Peshawar

1988 20 January, at six past thirty-five minutes in the morning, his last moments of life in the Lady Reading Hospital, Peshawar

As per his will, the deceased Bacha Khan was carried from Pashtoonkhwa to the provincial capital of Nangarhar (Jalalabad city) accompanied by a hundred thousand people and was buried in his own house.

Accordingly, he left the world to eternally rest in peace.

Pictures

Pacha Khan buried in Jalalabad

Ghaffar Khan's tomb in 2016, 28 years after his death

Ghaffar Khan's paternal home in Peshawar and his birthplace

Ghafar Khan's house in Jalal Abad

Ghaffar Khan with his son Ghani Khan, a philosopher and poet

Bacha Khan exiting from the mausoleum of Ahmad Shah Baba, Kandahar

Bacha Khan is meeting lots of People in Jalalabad

Bacha Khan delivering his speech to the people in Kandahar

Bacha Khan showing affection to children in front of the mausoleum of Ahmad Shah Baba in Kandahar

Ghaffar Khan and Gandhi worked & struggled together for many years

Ghaffar Khan and Gandhi were close together

Ghaffar Khan traveled to many parts of Afghanistan

Gandhi, Ghafar Khan and Gandhi's Secretary Mahadev Desai

Mahatma Gandhi, Maulana Abul Kalam Azad, Sardar Patel, Ghaffar Khan, Jawaharlal Nehru

Ghaffar Khan and Vinubhai Buhu planting a sapling

Vanguards of Nonviolence in Twentieth Century:

Martin Luther King, Mahatma Gandhi, Nelson Mandela, Ghaffar Khan

Bibliography

1. Abdul Ghaffar, My Life and Struggle, 1981, Kabul: State Printing House.

2. Pashtoon Magazine, Issue Number Eighth, 1992, Peshawar.

3. Eknath Easwaran, A Man to Match His Mountains, Pashto Translation by Ghani Khattak, 1993, Islamabad.

4. Abdullah Bakhtani Khidmatgar, Writings of Bacha Khan, Volume II, Danish Publications, 2005, Peshawar.

5. Abdullah Bakhtani Khidmatgar, Writings of Bacha Khan, Volume I, State Printing House, 1984, Kabul.

6. Instructions and Articles of Bacha Khan, Sayed Javed Ali Shah, Narshak, Classic Publishers, Nowshera.

7. Lights of Bacha Khan, 2012.

8. Honorable Memories of the Great Servant of God, Prof. Abdullah Bakhtani, 2011.

9. Instructions of Bacha Khan, Directorate of Publications and Cultural Affairs at Ministry of Tribal Affairs, 1988.

10. An Overview of the Thoughts and Historical Struggles of Khan Abdul Ghaffar Khan (Bacha Khan), Muhammad Gul Watanpal Dyani, 2010.

11. Rubies and Pearls: Quotations of Bacha Khan, Dr. Mohammad Zubair Hasrat, Pashtoonkwa Study Center, Bacha Khan University, Charsada, 2012.

12. Service of God, Khan Abdul Ghaffar Khan, 1965, Directorate of Tribal Affairs, Kabul.

13. Pride of Afghans and Afghanistan. Abdullah Bakhtani Khidmatgar, 2008

14. Two Servants of God, Mahadev Desai, translated by Zir Gul Wardak (Pashto/English), Kabul, 2017

15. Khan Abdul Ghaffar Khan: The Apostle of Nonviolence, N Radhakrishnan, translated by Zir Gul Wardak (Pashto/English), Kabul, 2017

16. Historical Speeches of Khan Abdul Ghaffar Khan, Vol. 1, Complied by, Abdul Rahim Bakhtani Khidmatgar, Kabul, 2018

17. Bacha Khan and His Struggle for Freedom, Atar Chand, translated by Zubair Zhman, 2013

18. Ghaffar Khan: Nonviolent Badshah of the Pakhtuns, Rajmohan Gandhi, translated by Ghulam Wali Noori, Kabul, 2010

19. Nonviolent Soldier of Islam, Eknath Easwaren, translated by Bismillah Pashtoonmal, Danesh Publications, Kabul, 2018

20. Freedom Movement and Bacha Khan by Farigh Bukhari, translated by Sajad Zhwandoon, 2018

21. Khudai Khidmatgar (1929-1947): A Strategic Choice, Ahmadullah Archiwal, Kabul, 2019

22. Abdul Ghaffar Khan; Faith is a Battle, Dinanath Gopal Tendulkar, Published for Gandhi Peace Foundation by Popular Prakashan, Bombay, 1967.

23. Eknath Easwaren. Nonviolent Soldier of Islam, Nilgiri press, USA 1999.

24. Rajmohan Gandhi. Ghaffar Khan: Nonviolent Badshah of the Pakhtuns. Viking, New Delhi, 2004.

25. J.N. Dixit, An Afghan Diary: Zahir Shah to Taliban, New Delhi: Konark Publishers, 2000.

26. My Life and Struggle, Autobiography of Badshah Khan as Narrated to K.B. Narang, Orient Paperback, Delhi, 1969.

Other Books

These books of Abdul Ghaffar Khan have also been published:

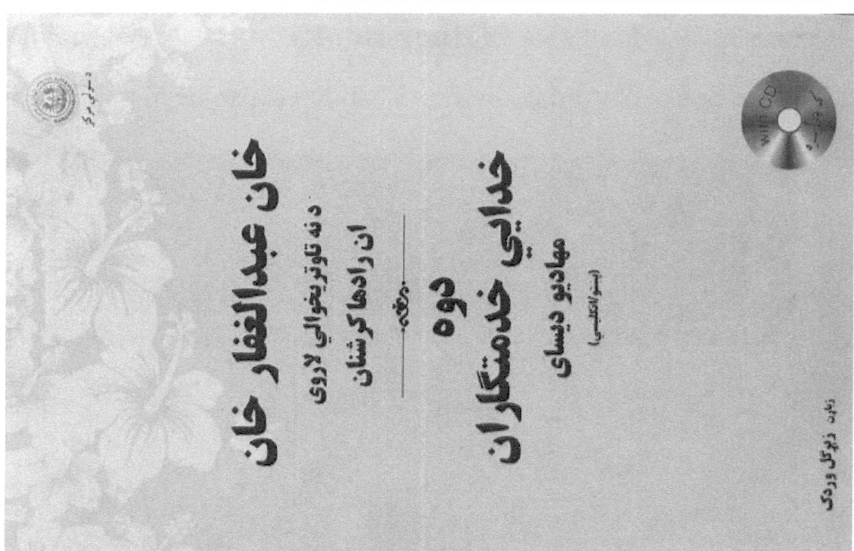
خان عبدالغفار خان
د نه تاوتریخوالي لاروی
ان رادها کرشنان
دوه
خدايي خدمتگاران
مهادیو دیسای

باتیں ہمارے
باچا خان کی

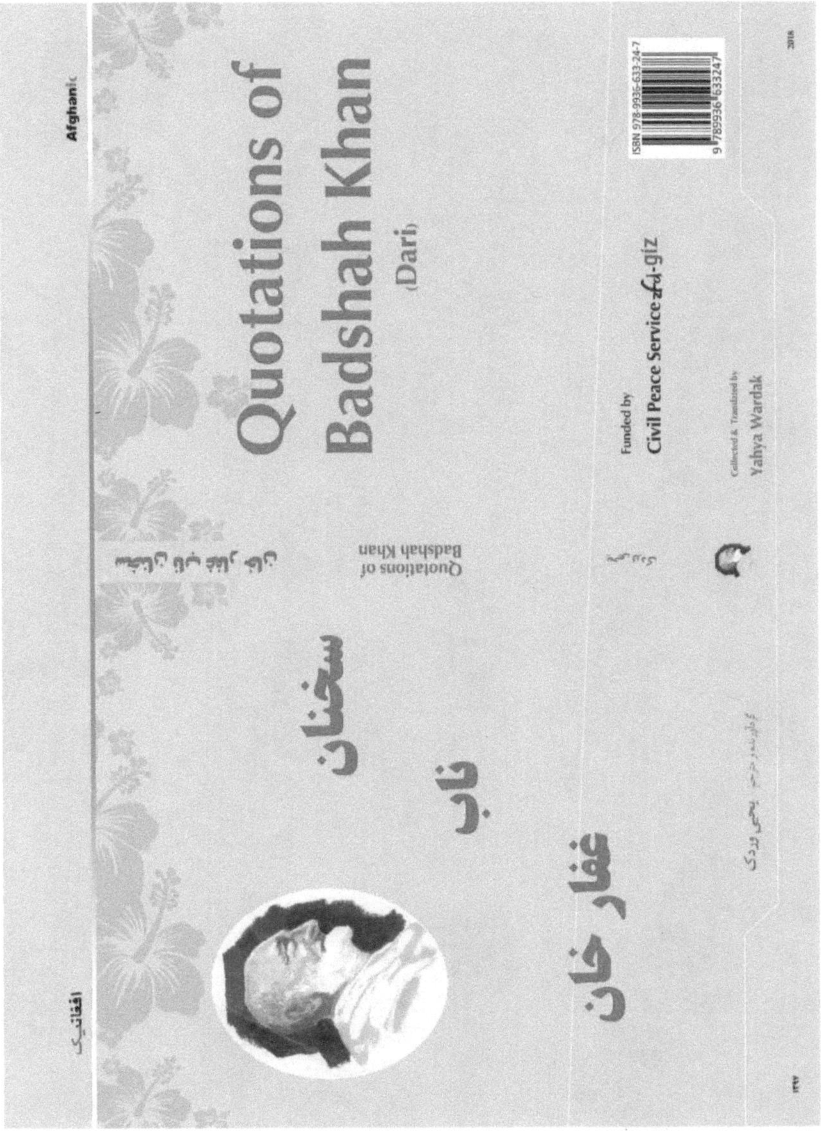

Afghanic

Quotations of Badshah Khan

(Dari)

Funded by

Civil Peace Service giz

Collected & Translated by

Yahya Wardak

ISBN 978-9936-633-24-7

2018

افغانیک

سخنان ناب غفار خان

Quotations of Badshah Khan

Afghanistan Information Center (Afghanic e.V.)

Since 1993, Afghanistan Information Center (Afghanic) has been providing information about Afghans and Afghanistan to the countrymen, associations, and foreigners. It is a nonprofit organization registered with the German Administrative Court. It was established by some Afghans and Germans to work and operate in Afghanistan and Germany.

The objective of Afghanic is to contribute to the development, education, and health sectors as well as to help Afghans in Germany and encourage the Afghan culture.

Afghanic has collected informative materials (books, magazines, newspapers, and cassettes) in its archive about important social, historical, political, economic, literary and medical fields. Most of the materials are the works and research of European, American and Afghan scholars who have studied different topics both in Afghanistan and abroad.

Examples of our efforts:

- Helping and counselling Afghans in Germany about language learning, life and finding jobs;
- Teaching native languages to Afghan children and teaching Afghan languages to Germans;
- Providing information, advise, and projects regarding Afghans and Afghanistan to Germans and German organizations;
- Holding the annual seminar of "Afghanistan Week in Hamburg" for the last 25 years;
- Printing the Constitution of Afghanistan;

- Publishing books about Bacha Khan in Pashto, Dari, Urdu, English and German;
- Establishing a health clinic in Dewanbegi, Kabul (www.dewanbegi.af);
- Printing over 366 textbooks of different Afghan universities and distributing them among all public and private universities; all of the printed textbooks can be found in PDF at:

www.ecampus-afghanistan.org
www.kitabona.com

Publications:

- Universal Declaration of Human Rights (Pashto/Dari), 1997, 2021
- Afghanistan Constitution of (1964), 1998
- Afghanistan Constitution (1964), German, 2002
- Afghanistan Constitution (1964), 2003
- Afghanistan Constitution (2004), English
- Quotations of Bacha Khan (Pashto, Dari, English), 2008, 2009, 2016, 2019,2020
- Pashto Learning, Manfred Lorenz, German, 2010, 2019
- My Life and Struggle, German, 2012
- Gulab Nangarhari Collection of Articles, 2014
- The Writings of Ghani Khan, German, 2016
- Afghans in Austrilia, Prof. Hamidullah Amin, 2016
- Two Servants of God, Mahadev Desai, translated by Zir Gul Wardak (Pashto/English/German), 2017
- Khan Abdul Ghaffar Khan: The Apostle of Nonviolence, N Radhakrishnan, translated by Zir Gul Wardak (Pashto/English), 2017

- Memories from an Afghan Village: Short Stories, by Zarin Anzor, German, 2017
- Publishing Textbooks for Afghan Universities, Yahya Wardak, 2017
- German for Afghans (Pashto), Yahya Wardak, 2018, 2019, 2022
- Prose of Gul Pacha Ulfat, German, 2019
- German for Afghans (Dari), Yahay Wardak, 2019, 2022
- Rahman Baba Peotry, German, 2020
- Higher Education in Afghanistan: Opinions, Suggestions and Advice, Yahya Wardak (Pashto/English)
- Over 366 textbooks for Afghan universities

In addition, Afghanic is currently working to collect authentic, academic information about fundamental questions regarding Afghan society and then publish it to be used by others.

In the archive of Afghanistan Information Center (Afghanic), a section has been created about Bacha Khan where informative material (books, articles, topics published in magazines and newspapers, photos, and videos) are collected and made available for the interested audience.

I would like to request all to support us in this regard.

For further details, please visit the following websites: www.afghanic.de / www.ecampus-afghanistan.org

Abstract

Quotations of Badshah Khan text was compiled from different authentic references in the form of a single book. It has been tried the best, during compiling the book, to choose the significant sayings of Badshah Khan which convey meaningful advice. Since Badshah Khan was a fellow of Gandhi the well-known Indian leader, especially regarding eliminating violence, each of his quotes is as a pearl to his followers who regard him as a successful leader. The selected quotations are effective in reforming the drawbacks of our traditional society. Badshah Khan spent his entire life in struggling for removing prejudice and violence. He believed in equality of humans, so he attempted to unify various ethnic groups and communities. Thus, his quotations are very effective in this regard, as well. At the end of the book, a chronology of Badshah Khan is written which indicates important events of his life, from birth to death. Hopefully, this compilation is effective in spreading Badshah Khan's corrective sayings to the society, and, hopefully, the society will take full advantages of the ideas of this honorable leader.

www.ingramcontent.com/pod-product-compliance
Lightning Source LLC
LaVergne TN
LVHW090131160826
845673LV00017B/1813